Circles *of* Gold

HONORING YOUR NETWORK FOR
BUSINESS AND CAREER SUCCESS

Vickie Austin

"Every relationship begins with some form of connection. We can leave those connections to chance or we can be intentional about both receiving and creating them. In *Circles of Gold,* Vickie gives both context and construct to being mindful of the greatest resource we have… relationships. Her specific roadmap redeems the art of networking by shining the light on how to make it a healthy way of life!"

> — JOHN G. BLUMBERG, CSP, author of *Good to the Core* and *ROI: Return on Integrity*

"A book that reflects the author—compassionate, genuine and truly helpful."

> — CONOR CUNNEEN, 2015-2016 President, National Speakers Association of Illinois, and author, *What Mark Twain Learned Me 'bout Public Speakin'* and *SHEIFGAB! Staying Sane, Motivated and Productive in Job Search*

"*Circles of Gold* is a superb piece of common sense advice told by a gifted individual on how to identify your strengths, organize them and then focus them on a promising and fulfilling career and life. In simple terms, it is a blueprint for those who dare to excel in the everyday business of living and succeeding. I recommend *Circles of Gold* with no reservations whatsoever!"

> — CHARLES LAUER, former publisher, Modern Healthcare, and author, *Reach for the Stars: Pursuing Success through Excellence and Decency*

"We'll never achieve our mission in life going it alone. No matter where you start you already have access to all the resources you'll need to get you to your goal. Vickie shows us how to authentically and honorably tap into our network and achieve our calling."

— JOY MEREDITH, author, *My Last Wishes: Life, Love, Laughs and a Few Final Notes*

"Vickie offers practical strategies that can help you achieve your goals just by honoring the people you already know. A must-read for people taking their businesses or careers to the next level!"

— BARRY MOLTZ, author of *How to Get Un-Stuck: 25 Ways to Get Your Business Growing Again* and *You Need to Be a Little Crazy: The Truth About Starting and Growing Your Company.*

"In *Circles of Gold*, Vickie Austin captures the essence and value of building relationships one person at a time—and she makes it so easy for you to build your own 'Circles of Gold' for success."

— BARBARA STANNY, author, *Sacred Success: A Course in Financial Miracles* and *Prince Charming Isn't Coming: How Women Get Smart About Money*

Copyright © 2016 by Vickie Austin

CHOICES Worldwide Press
615 W. Front Street, Suite 201
Wheaton, IL 60187
312-213-1795

All rights reserved. No part of this publication may be reproduced, stored in a retrieval system or transmitted in any form or by any means, electronic, mechanical, photocopying, recording or otherwise, without the prior written permission of the author.

Circles of Gold® is a registered trademark of Vickie Austin d/b/a CHOICES Worldwide.

ISBN 978-0-692-42171-0

1. Career success   2. Business networking   3. Self-Help

Library of Congress Control Number: 2016903654
CreateSpace Independent Publishing Platform, North Charleston, SC

Book design and cover by Rebecca Lemna, Lloyd Lemna Design.

*For my dad, Roger, my first mentor and coach;
and for my mom, Geri, whose "momisms"
keep me laughing to this day.*

TABLE OF CONTENTS

Epigraph
Introduction

PART I: IDENTIFY YOUR MISSION

 1 Find Your Place in the Universe *3*
 2 Getting Unstuck *11*
 3 Inquiry and Research: When It's All About You *15*
 4 Epiphany *19*
 5 Articulate Your Mission: When It's All About Them *21*

PART II: DEFINE AND REFINE YOUR CIRCLES OF GOLD

 6 The Power of Community *29*
 7 Keep Up with Your Contacts *39*
 8 Your 30-Second Commercial *47*

PART III: CRAFT YOUR MESSAGE

 9 Make Your Request—Time + IOR *57*
 10 Get Your ROI from their IOR *67*
 11 Prepare for the Interview, and the Art of Good Questions *71*

PART IV: CONNECT WITH YOUR CIRCLES OF GOLD

 12 The Campaign *103*
 13 Lather, Rinse, Repeat *129*
 14 The Gift of Gratitude *133*

Acknowledgments
About the Author

*"One's philosophy is not best expressed in words;
it is expressed in the choices one makes...
and the choices we make are ultimately our responsibility."*

— Eleanor Roosevelt

"Be yourself; everyone else is taken."

— Ocsar Wilde

Introduction

For the past 18 years, I've been on a mission to help people understand and honor the power of their personal networks. As a career coach, I've worked with hundreds of individuals who are on missions of their own—to find the work they love. The first and most obvious strategy in accomplishing any mission is to connect with the people you already know, right? But ironically, that's often the *last* place job-seekers look to connect. They invariably turn to the vast expanse of the Internet and the black hole of its job boards only to experience resignation and despair when their applications or cover letters go unanswered.

One of the questions I ask all prospective clients who are in career transition is, "Can you tell me about your network?" The majority responds with a stricken look. Many admit sheepishly that their network is weak or, worse yet, hang their heads while mumbling, "I don't really have a network." (This, of course, isn't true. Even monks living in a remote monastery, men who have made vows of silence, have networks.) Clients often express deep regret that they haven't been diligent about keeping in touch with the people in their networks, and they fear it's too late now to reach out, now that they need something. I assure them that it's never too late to network with the people you know—unless one of you is dead.

If you're one of those people who is discouraged that you let your network wither on the vine—if you've been too busy or too preoccupied to network, or you're just not aware of how important your network is—this book is for you. If you think networking is about "using" people or you've been reluctant to ask for help because you don't want to appear weak or you're embarrassed that you haven't reached out before (and you don't even know if they'll remember you), read on. And if you're under the delusion that networking is a tiresome round of handing out business cards at a convention or suffering boring conversations at conferences and association cocktail parties, this book is for you, too.

No matter what stage of your career—whether you're just starting out, a mid-career professional or a veteran in your field—the ability to build and then honor your network is key to your success. Honoring your network implies you know how important the people in your life are to you. When you *honor* your network, the people in your network never feel used.

I call these networks your "Circles of Gold®."

What are Circles of Gold? In order for people to be in *your* Circles of Gold, they must meet two criteria: They must know you by name and be breathing. That's it! In my experience, most people wildly underestimate the depth and breadth of their Circles of Gold. Picture yourself, surrounded by everyone who you know or to whom you're connected by common interests, pursuits, and passions. Maybe you're in the same alumni association, or you go to the same church, synagogue or mosque. You may know someone from the gym or perhaps you both belong to the Star Trek Fan Club. Your connections are all poised around you in a circle of support. And each of them has his or her own Circles of Gold and all of the people to whom they're connected have their own. So suddenly you are surrounded by people connected to other people, all of whom are at the ready, waiting to hear how they can help you accomplish your mission in life. They just need to know what that mission is—and so do you.

24 Karat Connections

When you're looking for any kind of resource—an accountant to help you with your taxes, an attorney to draft your will or a financial planner to help you with your portfolio—where do you look? When we trust our families, our finances or our futures to someone else, we want to know him or her personally—or to know that he or she comes recommended by a trusted colleague or friend. As human beings, we are risk-averse. We reduce our risk by relying on the people we know and trust to give us resources, recommendations and referrals.

Employers are just the same. There's an old saying, "It isn't *what* you know, it's *who* you know." This implies that our skills and aptitudes are less important than our connections—in a negative way. I don't think that's true. I think you must have aptitude; otherwise it's hard to compete. But employers are human so they, too, are risk-averse. They are much more likely to consider a candidate who has a proven track record, someone they have worked with before or vouched for by someone they know and trust. There's nothing nefarious about that—it's just how we are wired as human beings.

Our connections are like *gold*—24K gold. So why do we turn to the Internet instead of our own Circles of Gold when we are looking to advance our careers? Maybe it's some awkward form of humility. We may not think we know anybody "important." Although you may not be connected to the mayor or the president of a company, you are connected to a lot of people. And those people have their own Circles of Gold.

It's also true that we love to be needed—but we don't always like to admit that we have needs ourselves. This is another paradox in the game of connecting within our networks. I had a client who was a brilliant businessman, an entrepreneur who was launching a company that offered artificial intelligence technology to help companies market goods and services. He was reluctant to reach out to his network—his Circles of Gold—to get help marketing this new enterprise. Yet, when I asked him if he had ever helped anyone else in business or with a job search, he lit up like a Christmas tree. "Oh, yes!" he replied. "I love helping people connect." Why, I asked him, would he deprive others of that same gift? Once he reframed his need for others in that way, he was freed up—and he reported that he had a great time reaching out to his Circles of Gold.

So now you, too, can reframe your network as Circles of Gold that surround you, shiny and gleaming, eager to support you with whatever you're up to in this life. For the purposes of this book, we're going to be looking at how your Circles of Gold can assist you in getting what you want in your career. But feel free to use this framework for other aspects of your life—in love, friendship, spiritual mission or an avocation. The principles are all the same.

I learned about the value of my Circles of Gold the hard way—I got fired. Although I'd known almost from the beginning that the job was a bad fit, I stayed. And I stayed. And I stayed. What had me frozen to the chair? I didn't think I had a network so I assumed I was "stuck." I had moved to Chicago from Phoenix only recently but even so, I underestimated the value of the connections I already had made within the city and beyond. So once I was let go from the position (compassionately fired, but fired nevertheless), I was devastated, but also liberated because I was finally free to pursue what was truly important to me. I vowed never to hate my job again, and I made a commitment to help others "do what they love and love what they do." I then took a job I loved in healthcare publishing. I also began coaching other people part-time on career strategy using my expertise in professional services marketing, and my company, CHOICES Worldwide, was born. Five years later, I left my "day job" and became a full-time entrepreneur.

My interest in career planning dates all the way back to the early 1980s. I had been a newspaper reporter and I quietly quit my job due to what I perceived to be a lack of opportunity in the newsroom. I also knew, deep down, that I wasn't a dyed-in-the-wool journalist. *But what was I?* I had graduated *magna cum laude* with a degree in English literature, but I wasn't really equipped for the workforce. My husband and I had moved from Arizona to Lawton, Oklahoma, and my dream of pursuing a master's degree in creative writing faded as I adjusted to life in Oklahoma. I was a new mom and we lived in a community where the sole college only offered undergraduate courses. If I wanted to pursue a master's degree, I would have to drive to Norman, OK, which seemed too far a stretch with only one car between us, a new baby and limited financial resources.

Enter Edna Hennessee. Edna was a self-made woman who had been a single mother struggling to raise her children alone, and she had built her fortune by doing other people's laundry and using her income to launch a cosmetics business. Much like Mary Kay Ash (founder of the global Mary Kay cosmetics company), Edna had parlayed her knowledge and experience into quite an enterprise. I hadn't heard of Edna until I saw her featured in an ad in the *Lawton Constitution and Morn-*

ing Press, advertising a workshop called "Employment Opportunities for Women." Held at the old Carnegie Library, this workshop was designed to help women who were considering a return to the workforce after time at home raising children and the workshop included—go figure—cosmetic makeovers.

I hired a babysitter so I could attend the seminar and found my way into the second row. I don't remember all of what Edna said to us, but I do recall her red hair and her fiery delivery—she must have been influenced by a dynamic Baptist preacher from her youth. Here's what I do remember, almost verbatim, from Edna's presentation that morning as she exhorted us to find the work that was most meaningful to us, work that would make a difference in the world:

> "I don't want to hear that you can't do what you were designed to do, just because you're married."
>
> (*Busted!* I'd been secretly blaming my husband Bill and our whirlwind courtship and marriage for derailing my ambitious albeit vague career plans.)
>
> "I don't want to hear that you can't do the work you love, just because you have children."
>
> (*Bingo!* My two-year-old Kitty was a handful and, truth be told, I'd been surprised—delighted but surprised—by motherhood. I hadn't realized how hard it would be to pursue a career while also learning the ropes of being a mother.)
>
> "And I do NOT want to hear you say," Edna said, her voice reaching a crescendo with all the passion of a

Sunday sermon, "that you cannot do what God put you on earth to do because you live in Lawton, Oklahoma."

Well, there it was. She had found me out. I'd been blaming my husband, my circumstances as a young mom and mostly, blaming the fact that I was "stranded" in Lawton, Oklahoma, for my work woes. Lawton was founded adjacent to a military base, Fort Sill, and more than one person had expressed incredulity that we lived in Lawton even though my husband was not in the military.

In that one morning seminar, Edna Hennessee taught me the important lesson of taking personal responsibility for my choices and for my career. I went home, kissed my husband and daughter and went right to the library (this was pre-Internet) to study all I could on how to find the right career. Within three months, I'd landed my first professional job at a hospital in what was to be a twenty-year career in healthcare marketing communications.

This book is designed to help you with all the necessary steps in identifying, building and then honoring your own Circles of Gold. Do the exercises and complete the homework. Fill in the blanks and have fun. Once you've discovered and identified your Circles of Gold, you'll be able to tap into your connections with honor and dignity, gaining the support of the people around you. And you'll be able to achieve your wildest dreams, one golden contact at a time.

Let's begin.

PART I: IDENTIFY YOUR MISSION

1 Find Your Place in the Universe

Why do so many people resist networking? Why does the process seem so onerous that job-seekers would rather visit Internet employment listings than turn to the people who already know and love them? I have a theory. I think it's because we don't like to "use" the people we know and love, and some people confuse networking with "using" people. That's because their focus is on getting something out of others—some *thing*. That *thing* could be a job, a contact, a referral, or some other tangible object. Or it may be access to someone else within their friend's firm, so in effect they aren't really honoring the person they know. Instead, they're just using them as a courier for their résumé or as a conduit to the human resources department. This is, indeed, "using" people and there isn't much dignity or honor in that. But that's not networking, or at least that's not the kind of networking I recommend and champion in this book and with my clients. What's missing from most of those conversations is *mission*.

Each and every one of us is designed to want to make a difference in this world. Not just the philanthropists, or people working on advanced medical research or those riding their bikes across America to raise funds for a cure to a disease, but *everyone*. For almost twenty years I've interviewed prospective clients about what they want in their jobs and careers and—to a person—each one expresses a desire to "make a difference."

Perhaps it's in our DNA, or maybe we're designed this way to perpetuate the species. But I believe it's hard-wired into us, to want to make a difference so that we leave the world a better place than when we found it. It might sound clichéd, but I believe it with all my heart. When Steve Jobs and his staff launched the Macintosh computer, Jobs put it this way: "Let's go put a dent in the universe." The first time I heard that story, I got goosebumps. We all want to put a "dent in the universe," and it's up to us to figure out how best we can use our gifts and do just that.

Matching your gifts and abilities to the job market seems like it should be a simple task. Know what you're good at and locate people who are seeking what you have to offer, right? But it's not that easy. First, we grow up with expectations about what we "should" become when we grow up. Layer that with an educational system that separates us into groups early on—the technically inclined, the beauty-school-bound, the college-bound—and you have a whole new set of expectations thrust upon you. If you go on to college, choosing a major takes you onto a whole new track and by the time you're in your forties, you may find yourself in a profession or industry that feels like you're in a coat that's too big or too small. It just doesn't fit.

So our first step is to discover what your mission is. What do you really want to do? There are lots of resources available to you—career assessments, books, vocational counselors—and I encourage you to use all the tools at your disposal to uncover your mission.

Here's a simple tool I use in my own coaching: it's called the "Top Ten Things I Absolutely, Positively, Like NO KIDDING Have to Have in a Job/Career." List ten things you *must* have in your job or career, in no particular order. Maybe it's "flexibility," something I hear a lot from my own clients. What does that mean to you—

The Top 10 Things I Absolutely, Positively, Like NO KIDDING, Have to Have in a Job/Career

1.
2.
3.
4.
5.
6.
7.
8.
9.
10.

---

working from home? The ability to take off early to go to your child's soccer game? Maybe for you, it's "security," including a salary you can count on and insurance benefits. For many people it's working on a team of intelligent people who respect you and what you do. And for others it's having a boss who supports you and provides you with opportunities to grow. Maybe you want access to the break room or an office with natural light. Whatever it is, this is *your* list. Take some time to complete your own "Top Ten Things I Absolutely, Positively, Like, NO KIDDING Have to Have in a Job/Career." I tell my clients, "I don't care *what* you want; I only care that you get what you want."

Mission Critical: the Secret Ingredient to Successful Networking

Now, let's flesh out your mission. I think people get too caught up in what they want to *do* and miss the real point: *for whom* do they want to do it? In whatever capacity we work, we spend our workdays—somewhere between eight and ten hours a day—with a group of people. These people are either our "tribe," the ones we love working with and for, or they're not. The real trick is to figure out who you want to hang with during those long workdays. Do you love being with children? Are you lit up by helping seniors? Do you want to spend your working hours with people who love collaborating and finding solutions to challenges and problems together? When you imagine the people you want to work with every day, the people you want to serve, who are they? What do they look like?

We're designed to be of service to someone and your job is to figure out who that "someone" is. When I worked in hospital administration, I served in the marketing departments of several hospitals. I loved working with smart, committed people who were focused on providing healthcare services to patients. I get queasy at the mention of bodily fluids, yet I loved working in a hospital. The people I was serving were physicians, nurses, physical therapists and other hospital staff who were, in turn, serving the patients. Each day I was surrounded by people on a mission, and that made my mission a joy.

So what's *your* mission? Who is it that you would like to serve? Missions (or goals) typically include powerful words such as:

Help
Contribute to
Transform
Generate
Create

Fill in the blanks below:

I'm on a mission to make a difference by working with

_____ in order to help them

_____ so that they can

_____ .

For example, in describing my career, here's how I fill in the blanks of that sentence:

> "I'm on a mission to make a difference by working with <u>people in career transition and business owners</u> in order to help them <u>use their talents, gifts and abilities</u> so they can <u>make a difference with the people *they* want to serve</u>."

The mission statement for my business is to "create a world where people love what they do and do what they love." This mission resonates with most people because they want to love what they're doing. My mission may seem utopian, naïve or wildly ambitious, but it's big and inspiring and it gets me up in the morning. All of us need something bigger than ourselves to motivate us to get busy and get to work. That's *mission*.

Once you have your mission articulated, you now have the "secret ingredient" to successful networking. Let's face it; no one wants to hear that you need a job. We all need jobs. We all need money. That's a "thing." But if you tell me you want to make a difference in the world and you describe your mission, I'm intrigued and I want to hear more. And because I'm a human being who's hard-wired to want to help others, I may be interested in helping you with your mission. I may have ideas, contacts and other resources that could help you accomplish your mission. That's why networking is so powerful—it's a conversation during which you have an opportunity to enroll and engage other people in your mission. You get to build a whole team of ambassadors who will look out for you, ever eager to provide you with help along the way.

The paradox of having a mission is that *it's not really about you*. It's about being of service and making a difference in the lives of other people. Once you understand that, the world is yours.

2 Getting Unstuck

So how do we get un-stuck from the vicious cycle of resisting networking? How can we begin to see networking as the joyous, natural process of finding our places in the universe instead of considering it something to avoid at all costs?

First, reflect on all the times you've helped other people. Have you been someone whom others have called when they've lost jobs or found themselves up against other obstacles and disappointments? Think of ways you responded. Most people report that they love helping others, yet too often we resist asking for help ourselves.

Call it karma or a universal truth: *What goes around comes around.* The amount of time you've invested in others will most certainly come back to you. If you're stuck, it may be because you haven't understood the power of investing time in the lives of others so that when you need help, those people are available to you. And it isn't always the same people. I believe that just by putting your energy out into the world by helping others, you create a cosmic connection that will, most certainly, be to your benefit. Recompense is not *why* we do it—we help others because it's the right thing to do. But it's also a smart thing to do.

If you haven't been a natural networker up until now, here's an opportunity for you to start generating some energy that will come back to you tenfold. You can front-load your networking karma by doing the following:

- First, **answer every phone call.** Even if it's a sales call and you don't want to be bothered, call that person back. If someone is looking for a job and wants your help, take the time to talk with him or her by phone. If possible, meet for coffee and share your insights and, eventually, if you trust and believe in this person's mission, share your connections.

- **Volunteer**. Find something you're passionate about and volunteer some of your time to support a worthy cause. I've heard it called "time tithing," a 10% investment back into a cause that matters to you. Perhaps you can volunteer at your church, synagogue or house of faith. Maybe you want to help at the local animal shelter or food pantry. Whatever it is, your volunteer activity should light you up. Do it for no other reason than because it's a great way to contribute to the world.

- **Connect others.** Develop sensitivity, or a kind of radar, for hearing and understanding what's important to other people such as their passions, whimsical interests and convictions. Then introduce these people to others who share the same interest. Helping other people build their own Circles of Gold is fun, and it also positions you as a generous, powerful force in the world. Go out of your way to help others find what they need—a stylist, a babysitter, an attorney or a plumber. Share your resources like chocolates.

There are some other ways to get un-stuck or out of a networking rut. First, focus on your own health and well being. Whatever you're up to, your "campaign" to find the job of your dreams, get a promotion or create a new business will require willpower and energy. That means you need to be at your best. Pay attention to your health: exercise, focus on eating nutritious food and get back to your "fighting weight." Practice spiritual disciplines that keep you whole. See a counselor or therapist if you're carrying around baggage from a bad job or unresolved, painful relationships. Clean your house. As they say in 12-Step programs, do a "fearless inventory" of your life and clean out the clutter, including habits that may be holding you back. You want to be as light and nimble as possible when you go out there to accomplish your next step: Inquiry and Research.

3 Inquiry and Research: When It's All About You

The "Inquiry" stage is an inside job, and it's one that you've already begun by completing the "Top Ten Things I Absolutely, Positively, Like NO KIDDING Have to Have in a Job" exercise.

Now, let's look at what you're good at.

Write a list of your gifts and abilities below. These aren't skills—they are talents, inherent gifts you've been born with that make you good at your work. For instance, typing is a skill, but writing is a gift.

Gifts and Abilities

_____
_____
_____
_____
_____

If you're stumped and you can't discern your abilities and gifts, select a few trusted friends and/or co-workers. Tell them that you're working on a project to figure out your mission, and ask for their help. You can set up a meeting or you can survey them via email, and ask them, "What do you think I'm really good at?" Then, when they tell you what they think, *don't argue with them or disagree.* You asked them, and they told you. All that is required is your thanks, whether in person, via email or by writing a note. You can even send a gift—after all, these are your trusted advisors.

There are some other great tools to discover more about your own gifts and abilities. If you're near a community college campus, touch base with its career services department. Such departments often offer assessments such as the Myers Briggs™, the Strong Interest Inventory or the Ball Aptitude Battery® to help you identify your strengths, for a nominal fee. I also recommend the *Strengthsfinder 2.0*, a book by Tom Rath that includes an access code to a comprehensive assessment based on extensive Gallup research. This is a great resource and the test is based on the principle that employers should focus on leveraging employees' strengths rather than trying to help them overcome their weaknesses.

A caution about assessments: your test results will be a direct reflection of how you answered the test questions. In other words, you won't find a magic bullet or some secret uncovered. The assessments incorporate your answers and feed back to you a profile, complete with suggestions. The tests won't give you the answer to the secret of the universe or tell you what you should do with the rest of your life. That's for you to decide. The tests provide you with important *data* regarding your strengths.

The Match Game

Now that you know what your interests and aptitudes are, it's time to take a look outside of yourself and to do some market research. You're on the lookout for a profession or industry that values your gifts and abilities. In essence, you're playing a match game to determine where you would best fit in the workplace. I like to tell my clients, tongue in cheek, that market research is like asking, "Who needs what you gots?"

Market research can include primary research—going straight to the source—and secondary research, which includes getting information via the Internet, books, publications and other sources. Primary research might be conducted by interviewing someone who is already in the profession or industry you're exploring.

For example, just for fun let's say you think you want to be a circus clown. My first question would be, "Do you know any circus clowns?" If so, interview one. You may find that you love the idea of getting dressed up in baggy costumes with a crazy wig, a red nose and big floppy shoes, but you're not prepared to spend 300 out of 365 days on the road a year—and that's what's required of a circus clown.

So we go back to square one: what was it about being a circus clown that intrigued you? Maybe you want to work with children, make people laugh or be on the stage. So you go back to your "inquiry" stage to see what gifts and abilities you most want to use, then back to the market to see who needs them.

Secondary research involves resources you can find online, through a professional association or at the library. You might be looking for salary survey information, trends in the industry or companies within the geographic target zone of your search. If you're in business, you may be looking for demographic or psychographic information that gives you additional clues on how to connect with your target market. You may want to look at the local business journals to see what kinds of research tools they provide as well as any special publications they produce and events they host that would get you in front of the people you want to meet. Secondary research is a powerful tool to help you refine your search. Don't forget the gifts and talents of your fabulous reference librarian at your local library. Reference librarians often have access to data and resources that most of us don't even know exists.

You're looking to align what you love to do and what you're good at with an industry, profession or company that needs your particular gifts and abilities to accomplish *its* mission.

4 Epiphany!

By now you've accomplished the "inquiry/research" portion of your search and you have an inkling of what you're good at doing. You've identified your gifts and abilities, done the hard work of introspection to determine what you really love to do and for whom you can make the biggest difference. You've also spent some time doing your research, evaluating the market, the professions and industries that call to you. Eureka! You have an idea of what you'd like to do. Congratulations—that's a big step. A light bulb went on and you've had an epiphany about what might be next for you.

"Epiphany" is defined in the Merriam-Webster dictionary as "a moment in which you suddenly see or understand something in a new or very clear way." Perhaps your epiphany has to do with the logistics of a job. You realize how much you love being in the great outdoors yet you've been chained to a desk job. Or perhaps you have a special gift communicating with senior citizens but you're currently in a corporate role in a firm that doesn't feed your soul. Whatever you've learned, there's now a light shining on what it is you think you want to do and where you might want to do it.

By the way, you don't necessarily need to change jobs in order to accomplish your new professional goals. Maybe you're reading this because you feel stuck in your current job and want to move up the ladder (or sideways on the career lattice, another valid option) within the company where you presently work. Perhaps part of your epiphany is realizing that you don't need to leave your company in order to get what you want. You just need to find a way to articulate your mission and align people within your organization to help you. The important thing is you're now clear about what you want.

But having that epiphany is not enough. Knowing what you want and knowing how to get what you want are two different matters. How will you get from where you are to where you want to be? I say the fastest, easiest and most fun way to get there is via your Circles of Gold. We're going to put your network, your Circles of Gold, to work for you.

Before you can do that, however, you need to be able to articulate your mission. You've spent a lot of time thinking about you and what *you* want. Now it's time to start thinking about them.

5 Articulate Your Mission: When It's All About Them

If you've ever seen the movie "The Blues Brothers," you'll remember the line from Elwood Blues, played by Dan Aykroyd, who says that he and his brother "Joliet" Jake Blues, played by John Belushi, are on a "mission from God." Their mission was to put their band back together. Your mission may be a little different, but make no mistake—you are on a mission. You're on a mission to make a difference through the work that you do.

Why is it important to be able to articulate your mission? Because people are moved and inspired by those who are on a mission. If all you can share is that you're looking for a job, people may be mildly interested and a few may even offer to help but they aren't inspired because that mission—finding a job—is all about you. The most you might get is "Send me your résumé," or maybe just "Good luck!" But when you share your mission, you're not really talking about yourself. You're sharing a part of yourself that is committed to helping others, and most people love to help those who are on a mission.

Later on, we'll talk about putting your mission into your "30-second commercial" which gives people a sense of where you've been, where you are now and what your desired future is—that's your mission. Here are some examples:

> "I'm on a mission to make a difference with a company that is leading the industry in green technology."

> "I'm on a mission to contribute my skills in finance and accounting to help a healthcare company serve its patients, contributing to their health and well-being."

> "My mission is to align with a company that offers strategic counsel to firms that are looking to grow and serve their own clients."

The paradox is that none of these stated missions really has anything to do with the person who is articulating the mission—it's all about the industries, companies, clients or patients they serve. When you share your mission, your focus is on the bigger picture, what you can do for them. It's all about them.

People get that. When you come to them to ask for help with your mission, they feel like they are part of something bigger than themselves, not just helping you find work. They understand that your mission is about making a contribution and, like a virus, that's catchy—they want to be part of that mission.

I believe that we are designed to make a difference in the world, not just make money. Don't get me wrong—there's nothing wrong with making money. I'm all for it! But people are not inspired by our need to make a living. If I meet with you and ask for your help because "I'm on a mission to increase the contribution of my SEP-IRA 10% this year by growing my business," you're less inclined to be of service to me than if I said, "I'm on a mission to create a world where people love what they do and do what they love." The first one, growing my retirement fund, is all about me, me, me. The second one really has nothing to do with me but rather focuses on making a difference with others. Most people, when they hear my mission, are inspired. Who doesn't want to love their job? They know that by helping me, they are indeed helping make the world a better place.

Lest you think that's too corny or sentimental, I want to assure you that I'm a business and career coach and I live and work in the world of commerce. So yes, money is an objective. We all have to earn a living and I say, the more money you make the better since, in business, that's the game we're playing—or at least the scorecard. But for most people other than Gordon Gekko (watch "Wall Street" if you want to learn more about Gordon and the "Greed is good" 1980s), making money isn't enough, and it certainly isn't enough to inspire others to help us on our way.

If work was just about making money, Bill Gates would have retired by now. I'm sure he could have bought himself an island or two and he wouldn't have to work another day in his life. But work is about *purpose* as much as it is about making a living. Instead of retiring, he turned the operations of his business over to other people and now he and his wife Melinda are making a difference in the world through their foundation, "committed to helping all people lead healthy, productive lives." They do this both domestically and internationally through a variety of programs and the focus of their work, their website and their mission is the people they serve—not them.

If you want to get someone really engaged in helping you connect your gifts and abilities to the marketplace, focus on your mission. Let them know who you want to work with and why—what lights you up about that type of profession or industry? Give yourself permission to demonstrate some passion around what it is you're looking to do. That kind of enthusiasm is contagious and there's something about sharing your mission that invites people not only to contribute to you but to pursue their own passion and mission in the world.

When you're on a mission the Internet is *not* the first place to look. That may seem counter-intuitive. After all, the Internet is a vast expanse of opportunity. There are all kinds of jobs posted on the Internet, on job boards, by companies and within association websites. Why not jump online if you're looking for a change?

I agree that the Internet has a wealth of information and, ultimately, opportunity. But based on the principle that people hire and do business with people they know and trust (or with people who know the people *they* know and trust), I recommend you first look within your own network before going into the dark abyss of online job boards. Understanding and leveraging your network is our next challenge.

PART II: DEFINE AND REFINE YOUR CIRCLES OF GOLD

6 The Power of Community

The first step in honoring your Circles of Gold is to identify who is in your circles and then create a structure for communicating with them. How do you begin to capture all the contacts you know? Consider the various "communities" you are in. By "community," I mean *a group of people with whom you share, or have shared, a common time, space or experience.*

Here are some examples of communities:

- Companies you've worked for, past and present
- People with whom you went to school, from grade school on
- Fellow alumni—those who went to the same college or university, but not necessarily at the same time you did
- Faith communities—church, synagogue, mosque, self-help groups or 12-step programs

- Sports, hobbies, and special interests—the gym where you work out, any sports teams you're on, quilting guilds, a group of fellow ham radio operators, wherever you share a passion
- Volunteer activities—the animal shelter, not-for-profit boards of directors, wherever you donate your time and talent to a cause
- Your professional association (and there's an association for every profession, sometimes more than one)
- Your neighborhood
- Family and friends

For some reason, when identifying and documenting their Circles of Gold, people often overlook that last community—family and friends. We tend to relate networking to connecting only with our professional connections. But families and friends are the richest of all possible communities. These are people who know you, love you (or hopefully, at the very least, *like* you) and they are already in your corner, wanting the best for you. Please make sure not only to include them in your Circles of Gold, but also to keep them informed about your mission and allow them to make a contribution to you.

You may have more than those listed above. In order to get you started, please make a list below of 10 of your own communities:

1. _____
2. _____
3. _____

4. _____
5. _____
6. _____
7. _____
8. _____
9. _____
10. _____

Now, choose *one* of those communities—work, neighbors, hobbies, clubs, your professional association—and drill down to capture the names of 10 people within that community:

1. _____
2. _____
3. _____
4. _____
5. _____
6. _____
7. _____
8. _____
9. _____
10. _____

Perhaps you have a stockpile of business cards from previous meetings or conferences. Take some time to sort through those cards and capture all of the information from people with whom you want to stay in contact. If you don't remember who they are, discard them. Don't beat yourself up for not having connected with them while the contact was fresh. We are building your Circles of Gold beginning now and there will be many more opportunities to add connections along the way.

Now, go back and create lists of ten people in each of those ten (or more) communities you have identified. Your homework is to capture the contact information for each of those people, inputting the information into some kind of database. You will have at least 100 contacts by the time you complete this exercise. Remember, these are people you know, so they are ones you could connect with at a moment's notice. Capture the names and contact information of each of them so that when you are ready, you can reach out to them and engage them in your mission. Continue to add, edit and refine.

Keeping track

After I ask my clients to tell me a little bit about their network, I then ask them, "How do you keep track of your contacts?" They often give me a blank stare. When pressed to answer, they give a variety of answers such as, "On my phone" or "In Outlook." Some say, "I have a stack of business cards in my desk drawer." Others report that they still use a good old-fashioned Rolodex™. Whatever your method of documenting your contacts, there is no one right way. What's important is that your contacts are, indeed, documented.

Here are some critical recommendations for organizing your Circles of Gold:

- All your contacts need to be "captured" so you can reach out to them at any given time via email, phone, letter or social media.
- The information needs to be consolidated into one place, not scattered throughout your home office in the form of business cards or cocktail napkins.
- The system you use should have a function for tracking history and notes so you can document conversations, meetings and other forms of communication.

This step of identifying and then documenting your Circles of Gold is absolutely crucial. *Do not skip this step.* You don't even have to know what you want yet. What's important is that when you are ready, you can turn to your Circles of Gold to help you achieve your mission.

When someone gives you a business card, instead of throwing it into your bag or stuffing it into your pocket, take a good look at it. Honor it like the gold that it is. This is permission to connect. Use a classy business card holder to carry your own cards and store those of the people with whom you've connected. You can later add them to your Circles of Gold.

In the business world, this compilation of contact information is called a *database*. That doesn't sound very personal, does it? Nor does the word "database" reflect the kind of glow that the phrase "Circles of Gold" does. But essentially, that's what your Circles of Gold is—a database. You are going to capture and keep track of your contacts now and for the rest of your life.

Sound tedious? It can be. But there's an odd correlation between the attention you give to your Circles of Gold and your success. The more you tend your Circles of Gold —like a garden— the richer it will become and the more harvest you will reap. Think of it: what if you want to connect with someone but you've lost his or her contact information? You might be able to track her down on LinkedIn (and we'll talk about social media a little later), but some people don't share their contact information publically on their LinkedIn profile. Ditto Facebook. I've even gone so far as to try to track people down via the WhitePages.com site and, again, that information isn't always made public.

There are various software programs you can use to compile this information. I don't recommend one particular program, but want to let you know that there are several helpful CRM (Customer Relationship Management) tools including ACT!, which is the software I use to keep track of my Circles of Gold. Whether you purchase a software program or use Outlook or an Excel spreadsheet, the important thing is to capture *as much data as you possibly can* so that you can easily keep in contact with the people you know. It's amazing how often the strength of our connections boils down to the basics of having access to those names and numbers at our fingertips.

Here's what you want to make sure you capture:
- Name
- Title and company name, when appropriate (and this often changes over time as people change jobs and companies, so it's important to keep current)
- Email address
- Personal email address (again, people change companies so it's critical to have an email address that stays current)
- Mailing address
- Telephone numbers
- The source of your connection (how or where you met and other details about the ways you are connected). This is important information to document as your Circles of Gold grows; you may not always remember how you were introduced to a certain person.
- History—this is the section where you track your communication to document all correspondence, meetings and calls. This field is especially important when it comes to follow-up: "Did I ever send Henry that thank you note?" Yup—there it is, documented in the history section.
- Notes—here is where you can keep track of information your contact has shared with you, things you'll want to remember. Maybe it's information

like your connection's kids' names and ages; or perhaps you want to document that your contact is a die-hard Green Bay Packers fan. Keeping information about what is important to that person—*and being able to retrieve that information for future conversations*—is a critical tool in building that relationship. It isn't "cheating" to keep notes—it's actually quite brilliant, assuming you use the information judiciously. None of us can be expected to remember everything that someone tells us.

A Note on Notes

I keep a little notebook with me at all times so that, when I'm meeting with someone, I can jot down anything I may want to remember. I may choose not to write down personal information at the moment they share it with me, but I will often later dictate a post-meeting memo into my phone and then transcribe those notes into my database. This allows me to respond sensitively and with tact to personal situations, especially life events such as marriages or divorces, new babies or caring for aging parents. But the fact that I remembered to ask about a loved one's health or can remember a child's name is something that's deeply appreciated by the person with whom I am building a relationship. *Relationship* is the "gold" in your Circles of Gold.

The Care and Feeding of Your Circles of Gold

As you begin to build your database, you may feel a little overwhelmed. This is a big job, and it requires focus and diligence. It's ironic that when you're up to such big things, something so tactical, the minutiae of entering the proper email address into your database, can make the difference between success and failure. But think about it: if you can't connect with a person, you've lost that person forever in your Circles of Gold. If you have an email address, but you input the address with a "." instead of a "_" between the name and domain name (i.e., joe.smith@gmail.com vs. joe_smith@gmail.com), you've lost Joe forever. The care and feeding of your database is a critical component of being able to network with power and ease.

Over time, you'll see your Circles of Gold database grow. You'll update it as people change jobs or email addresses, and you'll continue to add information to the history and notes sections as you meet with new contacts and connect them to other people. Document everything. This will assist you in the long run, and having all that information available to you is well worth the time and trouble.

The building and maintaining of your Circles of Gold is a work-in-progress. Don't get frustrated if you think these tasks are never done, because they never *will* be "done." Your database is a living, breathing representation of the contacts you've had in the past and the people you've just connected with recently. Your job is to "seed, feed and weed" it with the same love and attention that a master gardener lavishes on a beautiful garden.

Now that we've talked about keeping track of your contacts, let's talk about keeping up with them.

7   Keep Up with Your Contacts

Whether or not you are actively seeking to make a career transition, it's important to keep track of your contacts—and keep up with them. As people send you email address changes, update your Circles of Gold. If you see someone changed jobs or received a promotion via social media, reach out and congratulate that person. Then make that change in your database.

The saddest stories I hear from clients in transition is they "forgot to network." Absorbed by their *jobs*, they forgot about their *careers*. I call this "gopher hole syndrome." When the earth begins to quake, when there's a merger or an acquisition of the company or rumors of layoffs, only then does the person poke his or her head out of the hole to look around and see what's happening in the outer world. Don't wait until you feel a tremor to protect your career. If possible, devote 10-15%

of your time to your career. If you're "giving 100%" at work, you're giving too much.

How do you make sure you're devoting time to your career? You spend that 10-15% of your time dedicated to professional development, networking and conscious planning around your career. You stay connected to people within your profession and your industry and beyond. You keep your network fresh and in good working order.

Here are some ideas for keeping track of your contacts and keeping up with them:

- Pick a name at random from your Circles of Gold and reach out to that person to see how he or she is doing. You may send an email or pick up the phone and call. The important thing is you're proactively connecting and sending the message that you care about that person. Devote 15 minutes a day to this activity.

- Join and stay involved in your professional association. I'm amazed at how often professionals don't even know the association with which their work is aligned. Associations are the easiest way to stay connected to your profession and/or your industry. Research, then join and get involved with, a professional association.

- Look at your calendar with scrutiny. How can you incorporate the time to connect with the people within your Circles of Gold and still get everything done that you need to get done? I'm not suggesting you ignore your workload at the risk of losing your job; it's important to take care of business. But networking is a lot like exercise—you can squeeze 15 minute increments into the day and by the end of the week, you'll have built some muscle. Likewise, if you take 15 minutes a day to stop and connect with the people within your network, you'll have invested an hour or more per week in your Circles of Gold. A quick email or a 10-minute phone call to a former work buddy to say, "Hey, how are you doing? I saw on LinkedIn that you changed jobs," builds the strength of your connections and keeps your Circles of Gold in good working order.

- Use the U.S. Post Office with abandon. Hardly anyone sends mail anymore. Send notes congratulating people on life events—job changes, promotions, marriages, babies, birthdays. If you see an article in a magazine or newspaper that would be of interest to someone you know, take the time to clip it and send it off with a note. After you've had a coffee date or lunch, write a quick note to let that person know how much you enjoyed their company. Keep stamps on hand and create a stockpile of good quality notecards and cards for special occasions so you can whip out those notes and pop them in the mail right away. This takes very little time and it reaps huge dividends.

- Use social media judiciously. LinkedIn and Facebook provide all kinds of opportunities to "reach out and touch someone," to quote the old AT&T commercial. Liking someone's post, sending a quick note of congratulations or sending a message builds that relationship over time. The key word here is "judiciously." Social media can suck the life and the time out of our days. Give yourself quotas for spending time online—otherwise you'll find yourself buying from the Land's End online catalog or reading the latest Hollywood gossip when you really meant to be building your Circles of Gold.

- "Woo" your Circles of Gold through special events. You're either in business or your career is just like a business, and businesses invest in golf outings, parties, skybox seats for the city's sports teams and other special events. If there's someone you really want to connect with, and a coffee or lunch date won't do, invite that person to the symphony or ask if he or she would like to join you on the golf course (assuming you golf, of course). I live in Chicago and I'm a member of the Art Institute, so I sometimes combine my lunch dates with an offer to have that person be my guest at the museum. We get to stroll through the latest exhibit before or after lunch or coffee, and it's a wonderful way to build rapport.

Keeping track of your contacts and maintaining connections with them is time-consuming work. Creating a structure so that you have updated information on your contacts, adding detailed notes, changing email addresses and job titles as people transition in their own careers requires focus and dedication. It's what Gregg Levoy in his book *Callings: Finding and Following an Authentic Life* calls the "pick-and-shovel work" of staying connected. I used to pride myself on being a "big-picture" kind of person; it has taken me years to develop the care and discipline required to maintain my Circles of Gold with love and keen attention. I also have an assistant who helps me maintain my database, entering information from business cards and responding to my email requests if I know there's been a change in someone's job status, email address or other pertinent information. But ultimately, I "own" my list. And I treasure my database because I know that the key to reaching everyone I value—from my family and friends to clients and the referrals who have helped me build my business—is contained in that database. That's why I call it the "Circles of Gold."

When you perceive your connections as gold, you begin to have a different relationship with the people you know and the art of connecting. When someone gives you a business card at a function, do what I've learned many Japanese business people do: hold the card in your hand, look down at the card, and then look up at the person. Card, person. Card, person. Make a connection between people and the cards they've handed you. If possible, write a few notes on the back of the card *after* you have talked to that person, but not in his or her presence. Reference where you met, note what you may have discussed and jot down any follow-up required. Carry a handsome or lovely business card case in which you keep your own cards as well as a place for the cards of people you've just met. Routinely empty the card case out and enter that information into your database. Sometimes, if I'm going to a seminar or conference where I know I'm going to meet lots of people, I'll carry two separate business card holders: one for my cards and one for the cards I'll receive from others.

In graduate school, I studied international management and learned that Japanese businesspeople would never dream of shoving someone's business card into their pockets, especially their back pockets which would signal disrespect. Do not fold, bend or mutilate the card, especially in front of the person who gave it to you. I remember watching, horrified, as someone who had just accepted my business card slowly curled it around his finger, turning it into a cylinder while absent-mindedly talking with me at a chamber of commerce event. When we were done talking, I gently slipped him another card, not to shame him but to make sure he had a card he could use.

A Note on Business Cards

Perhaps business card exchanges are becoming less common; certainly people are making connections via LinkedIn and other social media, and some people simply text their information from one smartphone to another. But business cards are still used to exchange contact information, especially at meetings and professional conferences.

Here are some idiosyncrasies related to business cards and how to handle them:

- Some people have so much information crammed on their business cards that there is no room for you to make notes for reference later. If that's the case, jot down the context of the connection or a physical description of the person on a sticky note and attach it to the card.

- Likewise, some people print their cards on high gloss stock. The coating on the business card is impossible to write on—again, sticky notes come in handy in order to capture the information I need to include when the card information goes into my database.

- I've heard people swear by the use of business card scanners that transfer information from business cards directly into their databases. I haven't used one but appreciate that for many people, this is an alternative to paying someone to input the data.

- Every so often you'll come across someone whose ingenuity compelled him or her to create a business card that is outside the norm—in other words, it's bigger than the standard card and won't fit into your business card holder. I appreciate expressions of creativity, so rather than curse them or defile the design of their cards I put such cards into a folder or pocket and add them to my collection when it's time to glean the data.

This discussion of the handling and storage of business cards may seem trivial to you. Trust me, it's not. If you lose a new connection's card, chances are you lose the contact. And without the contact, you can't build the relationship. As much as I pride myself on being a "big picture" person, I have learned to take great satisfaction in drilling down to the tiny detail of recognizing the power of those cards and their infinite possibilities. Business cards represent the person I've just met, and I honor cards as I honor people, handling them with respect and treating them like the gold that they truly are.

8 Your 30-Second Commercial

So now you know what you want—you've articulated your mission. And you're clear about the power of your Circles of Gold. You've created a database that is filled with gold, and all the people you know who are dying to be of service to you. (They really are—they just don't know it yet.) Now, you will begin reaching out to those people to ask them for help so you can accomplish your mission. But what will you say?

This is where a lot of people get hung up. They feel awkward, thinking that networking is asking for favors. People say, "I don't want to 'use' people." To which I reply, "Then don't." You know the difference between asking for help and "using" people. We love to help people who are on a mission, who are up to big things. If you approach people with appreciation and gratitude, and an understanding that you are available to help them if they ever need you, then networking is a graceful dance.

Without actually scripting your message word-for-word, it's important to come up with what you are going to say to people—after all, how can they help you if they don't understand what you want or need?

You've probably heard of the "30-second commercial." Sometimes it's called an "elevator pitch." Some people consider 30-second commercials the chance to wow or impress people with who they are and all they've done. Worse, some people see it as a challenge to cram as much detail as possible from their résumés into thirty seconds. Those are the people who feel obliged to share all they've done and all the places they've worked as well as statistics like how much they increased sales, volume, profits, all in less than a minute. That, in my opinion, is the worst type of 30-second commercial—and it usually takes more like thirty minutes. Your 30-second commercial is designed to give a *very brief* overview of what you're up to and what you may be asking for. You are "teeing up," as they say in golf, for a future conversation.

My version of the 30-second commercial is a simple formula:

	Your Past
+	Your Present
+	Your Desired Future (Mission)
=	Your Request to Meet and Ask for their Ideas, Opinions and Recommendations

The biggest mistake most people make in sharing their 30-second commercial is that they mostly focus on the *past*. "I've done this, I've done that, I worked here, I worked there" until the listener's eyes glaze over. The truth is, when we're listening to other people, we can only absorb so much information and if it's *all about them*, we start to tune them out. We're listening and asking ourselves, "Why are you telling me this? Where do I fit in? What's in it for me?"

My formula for your 30-second commercial is designed to move people swiftly from your past into your present, then quickly to paint a picture of your mission which is where people get connected to you. If your mission is big enough and inspiring enough, the listener is going to begin to think, "Hmm...how can I help with this mission?" You're setting up a scenario so that the listener will be willing to fulfill your request, which is a commitment to meet with you, a contribution of his or her *time* and, later, a contribution to your mission in the form of ideas, opinions and recommendations. You want to move the narrative quickly from the past to a conversation about how the other person can help you accomplish your mission in the future.

Don't Get Stuck in the Past

One of the biggest mistakes people make in delivering their 30-second commercial is they get stuck in the past. They either go too deep, going so far back in time that they lose the listener, or they get "hooked" by a time in their past which they haven't adequately resolved. This is one of the dangers of a 30-second commercial—it really is supposed to be thirty seconds, not thirty minutes. But if you've ever been to a networking roundtable where someone wasn't effectively schooled in this process, you know what it feels like to be held hostage by someone else's story.

When people go too deep, it's usually because they feel like they have to account for every detail of their careers. These are the people who essentially try to cram their résumés into thirty seconds. They may speak really fast in order to get everything in, so your head is spinning just from listening. These people also try to incorporate all the highlights of their careers to duly impress: you'll hear a rat-a-tat-tat of statistics, including percentage of increase in sales, decreased expenses, revenue generated, and so on. But instead, these numbers fall on deaf (or, by now, numb) ears. Without context, these accomplishments sound like empty bragging.

When people aren't comfortable with the way they left their jobs, their 30-second commercials becomes diatribes. Maybe they got laid off, in which case you'll hear rants against former employers. Perhaps they blame bad bosses and you're now resigned to hearing horror stories about how they were mistreated, misunderstood and maligned. The grievances may be completely justifiable; however, this is not the time or the place to air them. In fact, I often recommend to my clients that they seek the services of a good therapist or grief counselor in order to process what's happened in the past. Otherwise they just lug around those hurts, resentments or grudges that get in the way of being able to identify or articulate their missions. In short, when you're schlepping the past around with you like old baggage, there isn't any room for the future.

Back in the days of black-and-white television there was a show called "Dragnet." This police show featured an actor named Jack Webb who had a flat, monotone voice and played a character named Joe Friday. Whenever he interviewed a witness, Friday would say, "Just the facts, ma'am." That's the way you want to deliver that up-front portion of your 30-second commercial. Just the facts, please.

Be content with the idea that you won't be able to fit all of your accomplishments into your commercial. There will be plenty of time for sharing your achievements later when you're having an informational conversation or, God willing, an interview for a job or contract. The 30-second commercial is like a movie trailer or a "teaser," designed to set the stage, tantalize and generate curiosity. By the end of your 30-second commercial, the listener wants to know more. At least, that's the goal.

Your synopsis of the past can go back to childhood. "I was always interested in science," you might begin, and reference your education. "So I studied biology at Northwestern." Then take the listener into the story of your career: "I ended up doing research for biotech companies." Here's where you can impress your listener with the names of the companies you've worked for, especially if those company names are recognizable. If not, you may want to paraphrase with something like, "I worked for a small, family-owned firm" to give the listener some idea of your experience. Graduate education and transitions in professions or industries can be woven into this part of your 30-second commercial in order to bring the listener up to speed on where you are now: the present.

Being Present in the Present

This part of your 30-second commercial also needs to be drama-free. "I'm currently in career transition" is perfectly adequate for the bridge between your story about your past and your vision for the future. If you're still working, let the listener know that: "I work at Abbott Labs in their research and development department." People may want to know why you are looking for a job if you're currently employed: they may, in fact, be digging for the dirt. Don't get trapped by that. Remember Joe Friday, and just focus on the facts. What you can admit is that you are currently "exploring," "investigating," "doing research" or "curious" about a field or industry in an effort to learn more about the marketplace. No one will fault you for exploring what might be next for you. In fact, most people will be impressed that you're doing research before you are in a position of necessity.

Benign verbs such as "explore" or "investigate" take the pressure off your listeners. You aren't hitting them up for a job and you're not exploiting them or their Circles of Gold in order to get something. You are on a mission to learn, and that's appealing to most people. There is no harm in investigating. Compare it to going to the library—you can check out a book to learn more about an industry or a profession and there's no harm in checking out a book. In fact, the more you know and learn, the more educated you'll be should you choose to make a change. Research is a critical component in career development, yet often people skip this stage and start looking for a job when they get itchy or dissatisfied. And being asked, "Hey, I need a job—do you know anybody?" isn't nearly as beguiling as being asked to help someone conduct research.

So you've synopsized your past in a clear, concise and drama-free way. You've shared your present and said that you're currently exploring a transition. Now is the time to take the listener with you on a time travel journey into the future—toward your mission.

Mission Control—Taking Your Listener into the Future

Just like a rocket poised for take-off, your mission should be powerful, compelling and jet-fueled to take the listener off into the future with you. When you're sharing your 30-second commercial, be sure to use the connector word "and" instead of "but."

Here's how it flows: "I've done *that* and I'm currently doing *this. And now,* my mission is to make a difference by doing something new." If you use a "but" to connect your present to the future, you disrupt the thinking of your listeners—the word acts as a barrier or hurdle they have to get past to understand your new mission. Using the word "and" glides them from the past to the present and all the way into the future along with you.

PART III: CRAFT YOUR MESSAGE

9 Make Your Request — Time + IOR

You've done a great job of setting the stage with your 30-second commercial. The person you're speaking with understands the context of where you've been, where you are now and where you'd like to be. Remember, this is someone from your Circles of Gold, so you already have some connection or affinity. But he or she will start to wonder why you're sharing all of this information and history. What is it, exactly, that you need?

Your first request is for *time*. This is not a trivial matter, as my old accounting professor used to say. Our time is our most precious commodity—it's irreplaceable. When we ask for the gift of someone's time, we are asking for something he or she will never get back. That's why I believe that learning the art of networking is so important. By honoring people's time, we honor *them*. Whether we are making plans to meet for coffee or asking our contacts out to lunch, we are asking people to forego whatever else they could be doing to focus on us and on our missions. I often ask people for "the wisdom of their counsel," letting them know how much I value what they have to say.

When asking for someone's time, please never, ever use the phrase, "I'd like to pick your brain." This is a hackneyed phrase that is, I believe, both offensive and off-putting. Perhaps it's because I worked in healthcare, but the very words "pick your brain" make me shudder. Not only does the phrase conjure up a grisly image of a painful procedure and gray matter, it also implies that if we get together for you to "pick my brain," you walk away with *more* brain and I walk away with *less*. If someone asks if she can pick my brain, I reply emphatically, "No! I need all the brain I have left." But then I'll soften my tone and add, "But I'd be happy to *brainstorm* with you. Is that what you had in mind?"

Your *real* request, beyond their time, is for their Ideas, Opinions and Recommendations, or what I call IOR. In finance we talk about "ROI—Return on Investment." Asking people for their IOR is what will give you your ROI.

Here's why:

People love to share their ideas and opinions. Let's face it: we aren't often asked for our opinions. Most people would rather talk than listen. So giving people a chance to share their Ideas, Opinions and Recommendations is a real gift. This could be at the research phase of your journey: maybe you're meeting with someone who is in a field or an industry you're interested in exploring. So your questions are going to be very personal. "Why did you choose accounting?" you might ask. Or "How did you get into the legal field? How did you decide on going to law school?" Our career choices reveal a lot about us, and most people are delighted to share their stories with you. And, in hearing about the choices others have made, you receive new insights that can shape and guide your own journey.

A word on opinions: I've heard it said that: "Opinions are like belly-buttons: everyone's got one." When you're asking people their opinions, you need to realize that they're just that—opinions. If someone says to you, "Aw, the tech industry's all dried up. There aren't any jobs in tech," you need to remember that it's just that one person's opinion. All you have to do is read a business journal or log onto a news site to know that this statement isn't founded on fact. But you asked for opinions, so it's important not to argue with your contacts. If someone shares an opinion that you don't agree with, just jot a few notes, nod your head and say, "Oh, that's an interesting opinion." You may want to dig a little deeper: on what are they basing their opinions? But you aren't there to debate the future of the tech industry: you're there to listen to new ideas and opinions. If a comment seems off base, illogical or something you've heard before, be respectful and just say thank you.

After someone shares his or her Ideas and Opinions, you've earned the right to ask for Recommendations. Sadly, this is where most people start when they think they're networking—they begin by asking someone "Do you know anyone?" This bypasses the very person sitting in the room, leaving that person feeling overlooked, a bit suspicious and maybe even protective of his or her own Circles of Gold. Why should he share that with you? What have you done to earn the right to "plunder" her Circles of Gold? Only after hearing about someone's background, listening to his or her story and asking for ideas and opinions can you then go on to make a request for recommendations.

If you don't know the person well, make sure you have some information about him or her prior to your meeting:

- Access biographies if they're available on company websites
- Research industry or company publications to see if they've been written about or if they've authored articles
- Use search engines like Google
- Ask people within your Circles of Gold who might know them
- Look them up on LinkedIn

What is it you want to know from the person you'll interview?

Here are some sample questions to use when you speak to a new contact:

- Would you tell me about your own career path?
- Now that you know about my mission, do you have any ideas for me on how to proceed?
- What do you think of my strategy?
- What would you do if you were in my shoes?

After asking these specific questions, ask whether there are additional resources you might explore.

Recommendations come in two forms: people and resources. Start by discussing resources. For instance, you could ask, "Is there a professional association in the field of accounting that might be useful to me as I explore whether this is the right industry for me?" Or, "Are there any resources you could recommend that might help me with my mission?" Books, workshops, seminars, websites, webinars are resources that someone might suggest as you gently request help and recommendations.

Lastly, you can add, "Are there any people you recommend I contact to learn more about the field?" If you've listened deeply and asked good questions, recommendations may come up naturally. Be very careful and respectful. If a new name comes up, perhaps that of an accountant whom your contact thinks might be willing to talk with you about your interest in accounting, always ask for a recommendation for how you should contact that person. And then be sure to ask for permission to use your contact's name if you reach out. This is critical—you don't want to "name drop" and then have it get back to the person that you used their name as entrée. You can be sure it *will* get back to them, and then that person may be reluctant to grant you access in the future. Our names are our social currency, like gold. Don't spend other people's gold without their permission.

There's another reason to ask people for their Ideas, Opinions and Recommendations. By asking people for their help with your strategy, you have now engaged them in your mission. They've invested the time to share with you about their own experiences, told some stories, perhaps recommended people from their own Circles of Gold with whom you might connect. They are now "ambassadors" who are willing to work on your behalf. If your mission is compelling (and of course, it is—you want to make a difference with others and that's inspiring) they will remember it and as they come across people or resources that might help you accomplish your mission—they may pick up the phone, send an email or drop an article in the mail to you. Your job is to be open to all the contributions they want to make to you, even if they don't quite fit your picture of what you were asking for. Your thanks, as you acknowledge their kindness, is all that's required.

The best-case scenario is when someone offers to make an introduction on your behalf. This is something that expert networkers do with joy and ease. I love to make "virtual introductions" when I see that there are ways in which two people can be useful to each other.

For instance, I recently made a virtual introduction between a new colleague, Ellen, another business entrepreneur, and Monica, an attorney and the executive director of a state science council. Monica had recently hosted an event for prospective associate board members, people interested in supporting the mission of her organization.

Not long after that meeting, I met with Ellen who shared that she is on a similar advisory council for Fermi National Accelerator Laboratory ("Fermilab"), America's premier particle physics laboratory based in the western suburbs of Chicago. This advisory council sounded like it had been established for quite a while, so I asked Ellen if I could introduce her to Monica so Ellen could share about her experience with the advisory council. Not only would this help Monica shape her new council, but who knows what other kinds of connections and synergies could be made?

When I see a strong parallel between two individual's missions or interests, I am always eager to connect them. But first I always ask permission from both of them. Once I have that permission, I make a virtual introduction, either via email or through LinkedIn.

LinkedIn is an optimal method of introducing people, assuming both have complete profiles. By "complete" I mean the profile includes a photo—a professional headshot, which is absolutely imperative; an up-to-date summary of employment; and a career history. Skimming a complete profile saves me from having to go into too much depth about each person's background in my introduction. My focus is on providing context for how I know each person and then setting up the opportunity based on the synergies I see between them.

In the case of Ellen and Monica, I sent a virtual introduction and personalized the message just enough to give each a sense of the other person. Both are positioned as treasures within my Circles of Gold, and I emphasized the potential connection between the two of them. Now, it's up to Monica to get in touch with Ellen to learn more about her role on the advisory board. While my language says, "I invite you to connect," the onus falls on the one who is in greater need of information, resources or connections, and in this case, it was Monica. She did, indeed, reach out to Ellen almost immediately, and I look forward to hearing about their connection.

You've heard the phrase "Pay it Forward," and that's what connecting people to each other allows you to do, with no expectation of gain. Networking is all about bringing people together for the sheer joy of connecting those with similar interests and objectives. There's nothing more fun than knowing that some new project, business or relationship came about as a result of your introduction.

Laurie Swanson Oberhelman knows the power of connecting with her Circles of Gold. Laurie, an entrepreneur with both an IT recruiting business and a new life coaching practice, shared this story with me:

> "As an information technology recruiter for over 25 years I have a vast network of clients and candidates in the Chicago area. Many times I would have so many open jobs and would feel terrible because they were not getting filled as fast as I, or my client, would have liked. For many years I thought it would be a great idea to have strategic partnerships with other recruiters so that I could fill my clients' jobs faster and the other recruiter would make half the fee. It seemed like a great idea that, after several attempts, never panned out. Other recruiters did not want to spend time working on my jobs for half the fee. They had their own clients to support.
>
> Enter Linda McCabe. Linda is a star networker herself and had been a business coach for me in the past. One day she emailed me to say she had met a woman who reminded her of me. She was an information technology recruiter as well, in the Chicago area and had almost exactly the same amount of experience as I had. She wondered if I wanted an introduction. I was hesitant given my past experience but I trusted Linda, she knew me well and you never know, right?
>
> That was two years ago. Since then the other recruiter and I have collaborated on several different opportunities and we each have made over $50,000 because of this important connection from my 'Circles of Gold.'"

Get in the habit of looking for parallel interests and concerns between people you know and then, with their permission, connect them with each other. That's another area where it's important to ask permission. I always get permission from both parties before I make a virtual introduction. It's only polite, and it ensures context. I may not always know both parties well, so I'm clear when I make the introduction how I know the person and the depth of our relationship. Getting permission to connect people up-front is a critical part of the game.

10 Get Your ROI from their IOR

Networking is a lot like gardening: it takes patience, resilience, a tender approach, serendipity, faith and a plan. Although I'm not a gardener, I know enough about gardening to make the comparison. My sister-in-law Mary Pat is an accomplished gardener, and she shared a truism with me that all gardeners seem to know: the first year you plant a garden, it sleeps. The second year, it creeps. And the third year, it leaps!

That's very similar to networking. You may not feel at first that your return on investment or ROI is very satisfying. I've had clients come back to me with a disheartened attitude after having a networking meeting, one of the homework assignments I'd assigned. "How did it go?" I'll ask. "Not very well," they'll respond glumly. The client will tell me about the conversation and some of the highlights of what was said. More often than not, the person they reached out to *did* have some great Ideas, Opinions or Recommendations that the client just missed hearing. Or, the person sitting across from them didn't have an immediate response to their request for IOR. But invariably, they later got a call or an email from that person. The contact simply needed time to ruminate about what they heard.

Not every informational interview is going to be a "home run." I would say that you can look for a 90% success rate when you're networking. Nine out of ten people will "get it." They know the game, they understand the game is based on reciprocity and they'll be happy to share their Ideas, Opinions and Recommendations with you. That slim 10% may not be as adept at networking, and they may not possess the vision to see your mission. These are people who have what I call ALI Syndrome, or an "Appalling Lack of Imagination." Forgive them and move on. (Better yet, buy them a copy of this book!)

Like gardening, you can't expect an immediate return on investment the minute you plant a seed. Imagine—you're hungry, so you plant carrot seeds. Then you stand next to the little pile of dirt where you've just planted them, tapping your foot impatiently and waiting for those carrots to sprout forth so you can eat. That isn't the way gardening works—and neither is that the way networking works. Some of the seeds we plant today may not come to fruition for months, even years. That's why it's so important to *keep networking.*

It's also important to manage your expectations when you're reaching out to your Circles of Gold. Networking is an exchange of information and energy, and it's strategic, not tactical. Connecting with others is not intended to be transactional until there's an actual opportunity—a job opening or a possibility for a contract or engagement. Be patient and keep planting those seeds.

11 Prepare for the Interview, and the Art of Good Quesitons

When you're tapping into the power of your Circles of Gold, there are really two phases or stages of an informational interview. The first is the request—that's when you use your 30-second commercial to set up the conversation that you want to have with the person. But you don't want to have that conversation necessarily *right then*. Your request is to schedule an appointment so that you can talk with him or her, share you mission and your message and then ask the appropriate questions (asking them for IOR) that will lead you to additional resources and people.

There is nothing casual or cavalier about networking. The kind of networking we are talking about in this book is a powerful, intentional set of actions that move you toward your mission and to success, whether it's finding the right job or growing your business.

So preparation is vital. This isn't something you want to leave to chance. Elevate networking to the level of meetings and appointments. Be intentional about scheduling. Follow through. Follow up. And make sure that the conversation happens.

I had a client to whom I gave a homework assignment to meet with a businessman who lived in his building and learn more about his industry. When the client reported the "meeting" hadn't gone well, I asked for more details. It turned out that the conversation took place while both were picking up their mail in the lobby. This wasn't a meeting at all, and it didn't give either one of them an opportunity to connect. I encouraged my client to circle back and set up the conversation as a meeting that would give them both time to talk and get acquainted.

The Hierarchy of Communications

We have so many ways to communicate these days that it's sometimes bewildering to know how to begin. Generationally, we have different preferences for communication. Baby Boomers still enjoy talking to people on the phone, while Gen Xers and Millennials seem to prefer social media or texting. Whatever your preferred mode of communicating when reaching out to others, remember that your objective is to get in front of that person, face-to-face, in order to build a relationship. If we are sharing our mission, the most persuasive and powerful way to do that is to be together, in real time, preferably in person. I'll share a few examples of why that's so important.

I had a friend in graduate school who worked for General Electric, selling magnetic resonance imaging machines. An MRI machine today can cost anywhere from $500,000 to $1.2 million. My friend's work was based on a series of meetings with the decision-makers at hospitals, including hospital CEOs, physicians and the directors of diagnostic imaging departments. Ultimately, though, he had to get in front of those decision-makers to make his case for that big of an investment. I remember him talking about his many visits with the CEO, a nun, at one of the hospitals he visited in Texas. The sister wasn't going to buy an MRI from him based on a series of emails. He had to get on a plane more than once and go meet with her and her team before he got the order for that MRI machine.

Another example that underscores the importance of face-to-face encounters is the phenomenon of online dating. Courting has gone from something people did in college, at bars, or through the introductions of family and friends to the Internet. There's no stigma in meeting your beloved on a dating website. But, typically, a person wouldn't go straight from exchanging email messages to the altar. An email leads to a phone call, then to a coffee date, and with luck, to dinner. For some, that dinner date may lead to marriage—but not without a few face-to-face encounters in between. Trust is something that we build over time, and, let's face it, networking is all about trust.

So consider that networking in business, and for our careers, is a lot like selling an MRI machine or starting a romantic relationship with someone you've met online. We may begin in cyberspace but ultimately, we don't plunk down $1.2 million or pledge our troth without meeting the person first, face to face.

Here's something I call the "Circles of Gold Hierarchy of Communications," something I created to help my clients move their conversations "up the pyramid" to the ultimate, face-to-face encounter.

Let's talk about each level of the pyramid, starting at the bottom.

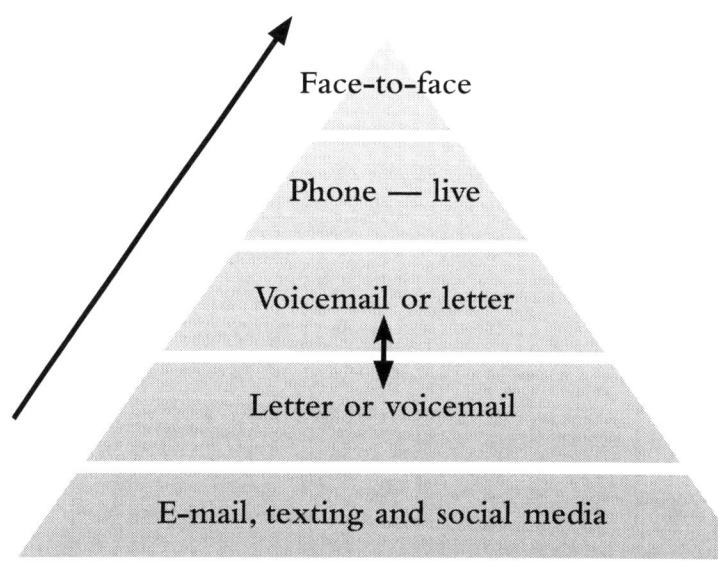

Circles of Gold Hierarchy of Communications

Email is so much a part of our work and family communications that we can barely imagine life without it. I do, actually, remember when email first became available. It was the early 1990s and AOL was in its heyday. (Remember America Online? No worries if you don't.) My family and I had just moved to Chicago from Phoenix where my mom and dad lived, and my mom, who was then in her late 60s, was always an early adopter of technology. She kept fussing at me, "When are you going to get email?" I remember finally having email available at work and the thrill of being able to write to my mom, almost in real time, across the miles. Now, of course, email is something we take for granted. Instead of one computer per house, we have desktops, laptops, tablets and smartphones that allow us to keep up not just by email but also via text, in real time.

But email can be perceived as "weak" as a communication tool. You can't guarantee someone is going to open your email, and most of us are drowning in email messages. An email is static and because it can only be read, it can lack tone or nuance. In fact, emails can stir up a lot of trouble if they are misconstrued, and companies lose vast amounts of employee time and productivity to misunderstandings caused by emails flying back and forth between co-workers. I call email "ephemeral," meaning transitory, brief and short-lived. Your email message can be deleted, whether or not it was opened, with the simple click of a button.

Using email, however, can be a powerful way to begin or to build a relationship. Email is probably best described as the "cover letter" of the 21st century. You can introduce yourself in an email, or be introduced as I've illustrated with the virtual introduction. You can position yourself positively with a crisp and professional message, or one that is warm and engaging. Your email signature communicates who you are, where you work (if you're using your company email signature) and perhaps some of your affiliations. I include the logo of my professional association as part of my signature, demonstrating that I am a member of the National Speakers Association, positioning myself as a professional speaker to everyone I email. Everything from the font size and color to your company logo give you an opportunity to position yourself and your brand.

An email is a great way to reach out to someone and then request the opportunity to take your communication up to the next level on the hierarchy of communications—either a phone call or an in-person visit.

This Hierarchy of Communications is built on the senses: with email, your only real sense (unless there is an embedded video) is sight. You can't touch an email, smell it or hear it. Again, it's easily disposable or, worse yet, can get buried in the mountain of email coming in from other sources. I'm always a little annoyed when people see me and ask me indignantly, *"Didn't you get my email?"* Yes, yours and a hundred others, too.

Texting. Once again, it was my beloved mother who introduced me to texting. She lived in Tempe, Arizona, where she was in close communication with my nieces and nephews. Once when I was visiting, the two of us were making plans to get together and my mom said, breezily, "Just text me when you know when you'll be ready." I stared at her incredulously. "Text you?" I said. I wasn't sure if she was serious, then realized she was, and I couldn't decide whether to admit that I didn't know how to text. This was also when I had a flip-phone, so texting was much more laborious than it is now. But I learned, and I have now come to appreciate the finer points of texting.

However, I believe that texting is a much more personal form of communication than email and should only be done when there is a relationship that is already quite established. My clients have begun to text me to confirm appointments or communicate the need to reschedule or that they may be running late. I take my cue from them and reciprocate when necessary. But I don't use texting as a typical form of communication when networking. It's more of an in-the-moment way of connecting if we are meeting that same day.

Social media. I love social media. Granted, I'm a late adopter (well, at least compared to my mom) but I've come around to enjoy the pleasures of LinkedIn, Twitter and even Facebook. Let's take them on, one at a time:

- **LinkedIn.** As I shared earlier, LinkedIn is a great tool for making virtual introductions. It's also a powerful engine for gathering information about a potential contact. You can see what people look like, read full descriptions of who they are, see what they've done by their career summaries and experience, companies they've worked for and groups to which they belong. You can find out what schools they've attended and whether they are active in their alumni associations. Some people are forthcoming about hobbies and interests, and if you study people's LI profiles, you can really get a sense of who they are and what they are interested in and passionate about. You can also tell how adept they are at social media: most people who are considered "active" on LinkedIn have 500 or more contacts.

My friend and social media consultant Joy Meredith (joymeredith.com) showed me the ropes of LinkedIn and helped me build my profile and understand how to populate the fields. If you are intimidated by LinkedIn, reach out someone like Joy who is savvy about social media. For the first months I was on LinkedIn I mostly just responded to invitations.

As a rule (and as recommended by LinkedIn), I never accept an invitation from strangers. However, every so often I will see someone I don't know but I'll see we have "shared connections," and I can tell from those shared connections how and why the person saw my profile and wants to connect. I will accept such invitations and then *always* send a reply, saying "Thank you for your invitation to connect on LinkedIn. Based on the strength of our shared contacts [and here I insert a few names of the people we are both connected with] I am happy to accept."

Now I use LinkedIn much more proactively. After I speak at a conference, I'll come back with business cards and contact information from the people I've met. I will send them invitations to connect on LinkedIn and send personalized invitations, saying how much I enjoyed meeting them and I'll reference the conference or how we met. I will invite them to connect on LinkedIn and, if I think there's an opportunity to take the relationship to the next level, I'll ask if they'd be interested in getting together for coffee or lunch or, if they are out of area, if they'd be willing to have a phone call to get better acquainted. I'm amazed at how easy it is to use this technology to forward relationships.

When I first started using LinkedIn, I had a policy not to accept invitations from people who didn't personalize their messages. However, I've softened my stance. Not everyone loves to write letters the way I do, so I've accepted that for many people it's standard just to hit the button that sends the automated request to connect. I do believe, though, that the best way to use LinkedIn is to personalize each message. A salutation and a reminder about how you met or know this person is critical to their ability to make a decision about whether or not to accept your invitation. You are, in essence, building a database and why would you want people in your database with whom you have no connection or affiliation?

Which leads me to another point about LinkedIn: it is not a substitute for your database. There are lots of good things about LinkedIn and it's added some bells and whistles so that you can input notes. The truth is, however, *that you do not own the data.* I use LinkedIn only as an adjunct to my database—for research, to see where people are, to learn what they are doing and to connect with them. I look for information about a contact before our meeting, seeking parallel experiences that might connect me to the person. Perhaps we worked at the same company or went to the same graduate school. You can learn a lot about someone by studying the groups they belong to—it says what's important to them, where they spend their time and to what "tribes" they belong.

LinkedIn is also the method of choice for many recruiters and executive search professionals to find candidates. I have one client who landed a great job that she still loves because she received the information via LinkedIn. So the communication works both ways—not only can you access information, but there's a "push" technology that actually sends job opportunities your way based on your profile. You can also do some deep research on your target companies with LinkedIn. Like any technology, though, it's just a tool. I wouldn't rely on it exclusively for a career transition strategy.

- **Twitter.** To say that I was dismissive when I first heard about Twitter is a polite understatement. I was skeptical of the 140 character limit of tweets. How much value could a person receive from such cryptic, limited communiqués? A lot, it turns out. I am now an avid Twitter user. I compare it to the Tao or a river—you can jump in, be carried by the current, and then leap back to the shore, and in the meantime you've gotten a sense of up-to-the-minute current events, linked to a great article that someone recommended, checked out a survey that supports a new project you're working on or laughed out loud at someone's comment or photo. I compare the character limit to the challenge of writing a haiku: you have to economize with words and that's a challenge for a wordsmith like me. But it's tremendously rewarding when you use it to connect with other people.

    For example, I recently attended a chamber of commerce luncheon and heard a terrific speaker, a market strategist, speak about the state of the economy. Bob was informative and engaging and when I got back to the office I looked him up on Twitter and clicked "Follow" so I could continue to learn more from him. I also "followed" his company. Then I tweeted a thank you, including the handles of both Bob and his company in my tweet, so he would be sure to read them.

    When Bob was introduced as the luncheon speaker, it was mentioned that he loves to race cars and that he plays the guitar. So in my tweet I mentioned something about "next time, bring your guitar," and I offered to sing. Well, a tweet-fest ensued—Bob and I connected on a level that never would have happened if we weren't both on Twitter. I would describe Twitter as fun, informal, sometimes irreverent and hip. And again, I'd use the river analogy—engaging with Twitter is like jumping into a river, and the Twitter feed is like a current that you are caught up in and swept away by. Then, when you've had enough, jump out of the river, dry yourself off and get back to whatever else you were doing.

I'm not as sophisticated as some Twitter users who consistently use hashtags to reference their topics or themes (#CirclesofGold #networking) and use acronyms and jargon. There are times when a tweet is so cryptic that I have no idea what it means. But many of them include links to blogs, websites and articles that turn out to be highly informative, resources for me or my clients and ideas for my own blog. So to those who are nervous or intimated by Twitter, I say, "Come on in, the water's fine."

- **Facebook.** Facebook is certainly a phenomenon the value of which—for a businesswoman like me and for my clients—wasn't always convincing. However, I can't argue with success.

    Facebook has the capability of creating a fan base that seems to exceed other methods of communication. There are many other resources out there to learn about FB so I won't go into too much depth here, other than to say that it's another powerful mechanism for getting connected to people. Because of its breadth and depth, I think it's the most seductive form of social media with the capability of de-railing one's focus and communications. You wind up reading about someone's summer vacation when you really mean to post something that would possibly generate interest in your business or next career move. Facebook is intensely personal and so I use it judiciously, mostly to reinforce relationships with friends and family, people within my church Circles of Gold and some clients who have become good friends. It's also a great way to see what's important to someone, but I try to be respectful and not a stalker or, in FB jargon, a "lurker." Participating in the flow of FB posts is important because it's very transparent—people can see how active you are (or aren't) on Facebook so just as in real life, you don't want to come across as using people to your own advantage. Also, beware of its addictive nature.

In summary, email and social media are excellent, powerful tools for building relationships, establishing your brand and connecting you to people with whom you'd like to engage. From a time management perspective, it's important to be disciplined about when and how to use social media—otherwise, you'll look up at the clock, it will be 5 p.m. and you'll wonder where your day went.

Letter or voicemail; voicemail or letter. Why do I put those two as interchangeable on the Circles of Gold Hierarchy of Communications? Because I believe that letters and voicemail are the next most powerful way to communicate, but one may be more powerful than another depending on your skills and talents. If you are a great letter-writer, your letters may connect people and open doors in a way that an email can't. Letters are tangible—you can touch and feel them. Depending on the type of letter (or card) you send, it can communicate a *gravitas* or seriousness about you that demonstrates dignity and class. For example, sending a letter on monogrammed letterhead printed on a heavy ivory vellum paper, hand-written and addressed, communicates an elegance that will set you apart from others. Think about it: when you sort through your mail, don't you gravitate toward the letter or card that's addressed to you? It's like a gift you can't wait to open. Also, although this may seem silly, letters are federally protected by the U.S. Post Office. You can be sure that, in most cases, someone will receive your letter (vs. an email which may go unnoticed or deleted.)

Letters are also much rarer these days now that people are so comfortable with email, so a letter gets noticed and distinguishes you from the crowd. The letter is a great way to introduce oneself; to ask for someone's time and attention in a follow-up phone call or meeting; to explain something that might be too long or complex for a short email; and to reinforce a relationship that already exists. Cards and thank you notes are a joy to send; they express your heartfelt appreciation, acknowledge the sender for a victory or extend sympathy or concern and just let the person who receives them know that you're thinking about them. Isn't that a great way to honor your Circles of Gold?

Voicemail is also a powerful tool and a message can be customized by the sender. Depending on the timbre of your voice and your imagination, you can leave a message that is lively, descriptive and expresses your personality. Be amiable when you leave voicemail messages. Give short descriptions of why you're calling. Speak more slowly than you would in normal conversation, but use your normal tone of voice. And for goodness' sake, please leave your telephone number with a slow, distinct delivery. When I leave a message on someone's voicemail, I always say my number as if I was writing it down myself—in slow motion. That gives the receiver a chance to write it down, too. Then I repeat it at the end of my message—again, slowly and very distinctly.

Phone—live. Getting someone on the phone these days is kind of rare. People always seem surprised when I answer my phone. Whether a phone conversation happens on the first try or you've set up a phone conversation as you would an appointment, talking on the phone has the benefit of being in real time. Plus, you can hear and sense the person by the sound of his or her voice. This gives you cues that help in building the relationship.

Here's some basic phone etiquette, some of which you've probably already learned but it bears repeating: First, always ask someone if now is a good time to talk. Even if the phone call is set up as an appointment, you might want to confirm that it's *still* a good time to talk. This reinforces the importance of your conversation and invites the person on the other end to commit to putting other things aside and listening and engaging in the conversation. If you sense they are distracted, it's OK to say something like, "It sounds like you may be distracted—would you like to reschedule our conversation for another time?" I've done this before and learned that someone was on a deadline, so we rescheduled. You want both parties to be totally present when you're on the phone.

If *you're* the one who is distracted, control your environment. Linda Klute from Tatum Partners, a member of the Healthcare Financial Management Association, talked to me one time for an article I was writing about the myths and menaces of multi-tasking. "I turn my chair around, away from my computer, when I'm talking to someone on the phone," Linda said. This allows her to focus on the conversation and prevents her from getting sucked into reading emails or being distracted by something else on her computer screen. I thought this was a simple yet brilliant idea and began to incorporate this technique into my own phone etiquette and protocol. If I am typing notes to track a conversation with someone (usually a client or someone I'm interviewing for a story), I'll let them know that's why they'll be hearing the tapping of a keyboard in the background. I don't want them to think that I'm answering emails or distractedly multi-tasking.

I used to have a dear friend and co-worker with whom, although we worked in the same office, I often spoke by phone. I could always tell when she was preoccupied or working on something else while we spoke. I could hear the tell-tale tap, tap, tap in the background. I would stop and say in a mock stern voice, "Are you multi-tasking?" She would swear she wasn't, but I could tell by her response when she was. Don't you just know when someone on the other end of a phone conversation is really listening or when he or she is focused on something else? You have the right to another person's full attention, and other people have the right to yours.

Using the phone powerfully and effectively is also subject to age and gender. Gen Xers and Millennials may prefer social media to connect; as a rule they seem to prefer texting to an actual phone conversation, something that perplexes and sometimes frustrates us Baby Boomers. I have found that some people prefer to use the phone with brevity and just to accomplish a transaction: get it said, get it done and then hang up. Knowing and understanding the style and preference of phone communication—or for that matter, any communication—of the people in your Circles of Gold is key to successfully building relationships with the people who will help you achieve your ambitious goals.

I've also begun to use video chatting as a way to make a phone call more personal because you can see as well as hear the person to whom you're speaking. I had a wonderful get-to-know-you coffee date with a woman from New York while I was home in the Chicago area. I had met Marion at a summit in Chicago sponsored by *Investment News*. We had a lively conversation at the summit followed by a "virtual coffee date" via video conferencing. We both had our coffee mugs close by and we enjoyed getting to see each other as well as talking with each other. Using live video is the next best thing to being together and meeting the optimal way—face-to-face. Marion and I later met for drinks in New York, meeting face-to-face at the Algonquin Hotel, the famous venue for the Algonquin Roundtable, and we felt like we already knew each other thanks to our "virtual coffee date."

Face-to-face. Here we are at the top of the pyramid, face-to-face with the person with whom we want to have a conversation. This is the person in your Circles of Gold, someone who knows you because you've shared a common time, space or experience. He or she is a person who either knows you first-hand or to whom you've been introduced by someone within your Circles of Gold. Connecting in person, face-to-face, is the way we build relationships over time, the way we honor our connections. Getting in front of someone and sharing your mission, then asking them for their Ideas, Opinions and Recommendations (IOR), is the pinnacle experience of networking.

Before you have that face-to-face interview, think about your intention. What do you want to accomplish during your meeting? What would you like to contribute? Walk away with? How will you keep the conversation and connection going after the meeting?

First, before you have that one-on-one meeting, I encourage you to think about and then actually write down "My Three Intentions" for the meeting. Let's say you're meeting with Susan, someone you met at a conference who is working in a field you're interested in exploring. Intention #1 could be: "Reconnect with Susan and learn more about her." Intention #2 might be: "Acknowledge her for her willingness to meet with me and thank her for taking the time to hear about my mission." And Intention #3 could be something like: "Build our relationship by finding ways in which I can support Susan on her own mission."

There is power in articulating these intentions and actually writing them down. Put them somewhere that you can reference them right before the meeting. Then ask yourself after you've met with the person face-to-face, "Did I fulfill on my intentions?" If yes, congratulate yourself. And if you didn't, ask yourself, "What got in the way?" Maybe you were distracted. Maybe you inadvertently allowed Susan to "hijack" the conversation so you didn't get a chance to share about your mission, nor did you have the opportunity to acknowledge her. If the conversation didn't go exactly as planned, don't beat yourself up. This networking game takes time and practice.

Preparing for your meeting with questions to ask is vital to having a great networking conversation. You've shared your 30-second commercial so your friend or colleague knows what it is that you're up to. You've asked for time—and you've gotten it. You've let your contact know that you'd like the wisdom of his or her counsel, and you've asked for Ideas, Opinions and Recommendations. Now this generous person is sitting across from you, ready to respond to your questions. What are you going to ask?

First, it's important to re-cap your 30-second commercial. You could say something like, "As you may recall, I'm on a mission" and then reprise your past and your present, segueing into your desired future and your mission. Then acknowledge your contact for being willing to meet with you and to share Ideas, Opinions and Recommendations.

Begin by asking about his or her career.

Here are some sample questions you might be able to customize to your own informational interviews:

- "You've been an architect for fifteen years. I was wondering, what had you go into the field of architecture?"
- "What about your work do you really enjoy?"
- "Why did you decide to start your own business?"
- "What inspired you take on that leadership role at the local chamber of commerce? And did it help your business?"

People love to tell their own stories. Let your connection share career stories with you, and don't ask questions that you could easily find out from reading LinkedIn or a biography posted on the Internet. Questions about chronology of jobs, titles and companies are typically available online. Ask the question "Why?" which is open-ended and gives someone an opportunity to tell you more about his or her specific interests, desires and motives. Another great question, formed more as a statement, begins, "Tell me more." You can take the conversation to another level altogether when you ask a question such as, "Can you tell me more about your decision to study abroad?" or "Tell me more about your role as chairperson of the diversity committee at your company."

Bring a notebook and two pens. The notebook allows you to take notes, and you may want to ask permission before you begin to jot anything down: "Do you mind if I take a few notes?" This may sound too formal, but I believe very strongly that it's the correct thing to do. People also tend to sit up a little straighter and think more intently about what they are saying when they know you're taking notes. They are, in a way, "on the record." I learned when I was a newspaper reporter that people like being interviewed and the formality of writing down what they say gives them a bigger sense of responsibility for sharing their IOR.

Also, feel free to write or type up your list of questions and tuck them into the pocket of your notebook.

If you're using technology like an iPad or tablet, have the questions accessible on the tablet. Don't be embarrassed to refer to them—you can even say, "I wrote down a few questions in preparation for our time together" as you pull out the list. They'll be flattered. I interviewed an administrative assistant once for a job at a publishing company, and after I gave her an overview of the job, I asked her if she had any questions for me. To my surprise, she responded in the affirmative and pulled out a list of questions from her notebook. I was so impressed not only that she had prepared in advance for the interview but with the quality of the questions themselves. Needless to say, she got the job.

I encourage you always to bring two pens to an interview because there's nothing more embarrassing than asking someone for the wisdom of their counsel and then having to borrow a pen to write things down. One pen may die and you'll have another one as a back-up. This is a small detail but one that is vitally important—it says you've prepared for the interview and you aren't going to miss a single word of what your contact has so generously agreed to share with you.

During an informational interview, the person with whom you are meeting ideally will talk at least 75% of the time. Let's say you're meeting for at a coffee shop, and the typical informational interview takes about an hour. Take a few minutes to recap your mission, reprising your 30-second commercial, and then begin by asking your questions five to ten minutes into the interview. Your prepared questions will get the interview

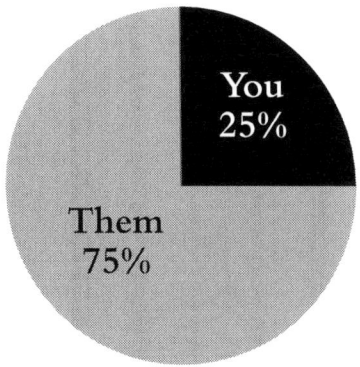

Ideal Face-to-Face Interview

going, and then you may hear things that will cause you to ask additional questions. Allow your interest in that person and your curiosity about his or her career path to carry the interview. Stay away from anything political or controversial—you're not there to grill them or to debate an issue. You're entitled to your own opinions, but that's not why you asked to meet. You're there to transfer knowledge and information in a respectful, engaging, and even fun manner. And you'll plant seeds so that if your contact hears about anything else that might assist you on your mission, she or he will be sure to reach out to you with additional resources in the future.

If you have a choice between making a coffee date or a lunch date to conduct your interview, I encourage you to opt for going out for coffee. Here's why: a typical lunch date is consumed with small talk to get reconnected then time spent poring over the menu and deciding what each person will eat. Then, typically, you may revert back to small talk or you may have a chance to get started asking your questions. But then the meal arrives. You have to put your notebook away in order to eat, and it's generally considered impolite to get too deep into business while you're eating. So you come back up to a surface conversation, which isn't necessarily bad—you just can't really document what's being said. Your lunch date may talk about her vacation, or you may have a chance to learn more about her family.

Breaking bread together is a good way to establish intimacy, but you just may not have a chance to go quite as deep with your questions as you wanted to, at least not until coffee and dessert. People often are pressed for time and have to get back to work or other commitments. Breakfast meetings are a nice alternative to lunch dates, too, especially for people who are morning people. You'll find that business owners and sales people often prefer early morning meetings because that allows them time to network outside of official work hours, so they don't lose any time that they could have spent making money.

During a coffee date, you have time to get into more depth with your conversation. It's also a cheaper investment, especially if you're on a campaign and you're meeting with five to ten contacts a week. Coffee shops are now acceptable venues for exchanging Ideas, Opinions and Recommendations, and I've even seen people conducting job interviews with résumés in front of them at local coffee shops.

The only drawback to coffee shop connections is the background noise. I'm one of those people who gets easily distracted so if there is music blaring over the sound system or a lot of noise from other people, it's often hard for me to hear or concentrate. I know I'm not the only one who has trouble focusing in a noisy room. I prefer someplace quiet to meet and if someone is asking for *my* Ideas, Opinions and Recommendations, I will offer to meet at my office where I control the noise, the light and the temperature. That may sound like I'm a control freak—and I am, especially when it comes to my environment. Controlling your surroundings helps you stay focused and present, able to hear what the person across from you is saying. After all, that's why you're there.

Staging an informational interview is a lot like choreographing a dance. You put a lot of time, sweat and practice into the preparation, and you want the result to look graceful and elegant. Just as with a phone conversation, ask the person how much time he or she has for the appointment. Lunch dates are usually an hour. Coffee dates might be 45 minutes. Say, in advance, "I want to respect your time today," and ask how much time she or he has to offer. If you're meeting someone in person or doing a phone interview, you might ask for anywhere between 15 and 20 minutes. That amount of time demonstrates that you are on task and that you don't want to be presumptuous. In my experience, though, as people get on a roll sharing with you their Ideas, Opinions and Recommendations, the interview that was scheduled for 20 minutes can stretch to an hour.

The Drive-By

There's another form of informational interview: the Drive-By. I don't necessarily recommend this method as it's random and you may or may not connect with the person you've targeted for an interview. But I had a very successful drive-by that led to a long and rewarding career in healthcare marketing, so I'll reference it as yet another way to connect with people in your Circles of Gold.

As I mentioned earlier, when I was in my early 20s my husband and I moved from Tucson, Arizona, to Lawton, Oklahoma. Bill had accepted a job as curator of exhibits for the Museum of the Great Plains. I had recently given birth to our daughter, Kitty, and I've often said that I moved to Oklahoma with a brand new baby and a brand new college degree and I didn't know what to do with either one of them. As I learned the ropes of motherhood, I was also casting about for a way to use my bachelor's degree. I found myself employed as a reporter for a daily newspaper covering healthcare.

That may sound more glamorous than it was; in addition to covering healthcare, I wrote obituaries and I also transcribed birth announcements supplied to us by hospitals. The newsroom where I worked at the *Lawton Constitution and Morning Press* had recently converted to computers but I typed on a manual typewriter each obituary that was called in by our friendly local morticians, generating hard copy on a continuous roll of yellow newsprint that I would rip off and then wheel around and type into the computer. I covered four hospitals—the big county hospital, a smaller private hospital, the Army hospital associated with the Fort Sill military base; and Lawton Indian Hospital.

When I wasn't cranking out obits, I responded to press releases coming in from the various hospitals. The hospital with the best news by far was Southwestern Hospital, the private hospital which had an aggressive outreach program. This was in the early 1980s and Southwestern had an active community education program so I wrote many stories about their classes on topics such as nutrition and stress management and I responded eagerly to their story ideas. My contact there was a beautiful woman who was cool and graceful and the ultimate professional. She kept in touch with me, fed me press releases and kept me informed about ongoing events and news by sending me their newsletter.

More than a year later I quit my job at the newspaper, frustrated by what I perceived to be a lack of opportunity for advancement. After a few months I was itching to get back to work and, on a whim, I stopped in at Southwestern Hospital to see my contact, Helen. I didn't have an appointment so I was extremely lucky that she agreed to see me. I confessed my mission to her: I wanted to use my writing skills in the business world. That was about as specific as I could be. But I had no background in business and, to be honest, had only a vague idea of what the "business world" even was—at the time, I didn't know the difference between a stock and a bond. Helen leaned across her desk and said, "I'd hire you in a minute if I had a job."

I was flattered. But really, I was just there for her Ideas, Opinions and Recommendations. I recently had read several books on building a career and I'd learned about the power of the informational interview. I'd read that it was a good idea to identify people you admire (people within your Circles of Gold) and share your mission and ask them questions that will help you get closer to your goal. So when Helen said she'd hire me in a minute, I barely acknowledged the compliment. I thanked her and then pressed her: *Really, what should I do?*

It turns out that her formal role was not as the public relations director, but rather Helen was the *personnel director*. She was doing the hospital's media relations only because they didn't have anyone else to do it. Helen promised to talk to her hospital CEO and, within a few weeks, they offered me a job as a communications specialist for the hospital. Within six months I was hired full-time as director of community relations, a job I adored and one that led to a career of nearly 20 years in hospital marketing communications.

All because of a drive-by.

Moving Up the Pyramid of the "Circles of Gold Hierarchy of Communications"

Each of these communications techniques—from texting and email to writing letters or talking on the phone, all the way to meeting someone in person—contribute to the development of a relationship. Your goal is to move the connection up the pyramid of the Circles of Gold Hierarchy of Communications with the ultimate goal of having the opportunity to share your mission and engage the person in your Circles of Gold in such a way that they want to help you achieve your mission.

PART IV: CONNECT WITH YOUR
CIRCLES OF GOLD

12 The Campaign

While I consider myself a pacifist, I can't help but compare a networking campaign to a military one. Not that I know that much about military strategy—my ideas about warfare are mostly taken from things I've seen in old black-and-white movies. I picture Campaign Headquarters as a big room filled with maps and Winston Churchill in a World War II bunker. There's a lot of plotting, discussions about strategy, and people are deployed—it's quite similar, really, to a great networking campaign.

"Campaign" also carries the connotation that it is ongoing, something that needs to be planned and executed over time. That's how networking is, too. Keeping your networking campaign going is vital to achieving your goals and dreams. Therefore, you're going to need various resources as you develop your business or your career.

These resources include:

A calendar system. Back in the day, a lot of people used paper calendar systems like the Franklin Planner (now Franklin-Covey), DayTimer or Filofax, and many still do. I recently visited a large office supply store in Brooklyn that was filled to the brim with calendars—wall calendars, academic calendars for schoolteachers and students, and replacement calendars for the aforementioned systems. Some people like to carry a pocket calendar; others prefer the larger notebook size or even a big binder.

With the advent of technology, we can now use an electronic calendar, which syncs to our computers and our phones. Late adopter that I am, I was resistant to this technology until someone introduced me to Google Calendar. I keep my calendar online, color-coded by appointment—yellow for networking, green for revenue-generating appointments, peach for administrative tasks, and so on. The calendar is available via my computer and it syncs immediately with my iPhone. I can make appointments on my phone when I'm sitting in meetings with my clients or with a colleague and they will automatically synchronize to my desktop. My assistant has access to my calendar via the cloud and she can make additions or changes as needed. I don't question the miracle of this technology: I just appreciate it.

The point is, whatever calendar system you use is absolutely fine. Don't let anyone bully you into changing it unless you want to. If you still use a paper system, keep some sort of a back-up so that if you should lose your "book," you know where you're supposed to be the next day. You need to be in love with your calendar system, because although we talk about making a difference in the world and honoring your Circles of Gold in order to do that, it all comes down to scheduling. Putting something into existence on your calendar is a sacred commitment to you, your mission and the person or event to whom you've committed. Your calendar will carry you forward toward the achievement of your goals. Tom Peters, the über-guru of management and co-author of the 1980s classic *In Search of Excellence*, is quoted as saying, "Show me your calendar and I'll show you what's important to you."

A database. We're already covered the importance of having a database, but it bears repeating: your database is the heart of your campaign and without one it will be difficult—if not impossible—to network effectively. Have all your contacts collected into one place so that those people are at your fingertips should you need to reach them. Keeping your database fresh and up-to-date is a work-in-progress and a job that is never completed. People move, change jobs and change email addresses. Your job is to keep up with them as much as possible. You may find yourself having to track someone down because the email you wrote bounced. A lot of people are getting rid of their home and office landlines and using only mobile phones these days; you may have to reach them some other way. Just know that keeping your database as current as you can is a Sisyphean task worth attempting.

Tracking systems. Keeping track of your contacts is one thing; keeping track of your activity is quite another. When you're on a campaign, the more successful you are, the more volume you create. And you want to document your activity so that you are able to use all the valuable information you're gathering from your Circles of Gold. You want to be able to remember when and where you met someone; follow up on the recommendations he or she may have given you; respond with a thank you note for the person's time and contribution; and circle back around with a progress report. The networking game is contingent upon "keeping the ball in play."

I remember the first tracking report I ever created: it was a Word Perfect document, set up as a table, and I made copies and collated the pages into a booklet. I'd been on a networking campaign with the objective of changing from one industry (healthcare) to another (the agency business). Thanks to my Circles of Gold and introductions to other people within *their* Circles of Gold, I had generated a lot of meetings and activity. One night I was lying awake in bed in a panic, thinking about an interview I'd had and wondering, "Did I ever send that person a thank you note?" I couldn't remember. I realized then and there that I had better create some sort of tracking mechanism, and that's when I created the Word Perfect contact grid. I included headings for the person's name and company, the date and place we met, a notes section for what was said and a large field for follow-up.

Cut to the present: there are all kinds of Customer Relationship Management systems (CRMs) on the market. I use a program called ACT! Within ACT! I can track all my contacts, beginning with when each name was entered into the database, birthdays, and even the names of my contacts' spouses or significant others. I began using ACT! almost immediately when I began my coaching business because I had used the same system while employed at *Modern Healthcare* magazine at Crain Communications publishing firm and I knew how robust ACT!'s capabilities are.

My first administrative assistant, Paula, set ACT! up for me. She was a former Lucent Technology leader who had retired and was looking for a place to make a difference. When I put out the word (through my Circles of Gold, of course) that I was looking for an administrative assistant, Paula said, "I have just the person for you." "Who?" I asked. "Me!" she replied.

Having Paula for an administrative assistant was like having an Uzi to get rid of a few ants in the kitchen. She possessed more technical knowledge and insight about database management than I could have dreamed. So thanks to her, my business began on the right foot because she had the technology expertise and know-how to help me purchase the appropriate computer and to load the software I needed, including ACT! My friend, and fellow member of the National Speakers

Association, John Blumberg also uses ACT! and he, too, recommends getting as robust a system as you can. Your database is the engine of your business and your career.

As I mentioned earlier, whatever system you choose, you want a tracking system that will allow you to capture all the information you need (name, company, address, phone numbers, email addresses) and also a place for you to document "notes" and "history." The notes section is for the personal information and the history activity section is for chronologically tracking your meetings, phone calls and correspondence. This is that critical field in which you will keep track of details such as "thank you note sent" or "résumé and cover letter emailed" and the dates the mailings were sent.

As I've mentioned, I describe myself as a "big picture" person. I love strategy and that's the world I'm most comfortable in, not the mundane world of entering details like the date I sent someone a thank you note. But it's also been said that, "God is in the details." I've learned as I've developed my coaching practice, and perhaps as I've gotten older, that details are, indeed, very important. I do have help in entering data—my current assistant takes the information I send her via email or on business cards and painstakingly enters it into my ACT! database. But if I forget to document a visit, a phone call or whether I've sent a thank you note, I'm left wondering, "Did I close the loop on that conversation?" The data is only as good as the information I take the time to enter. So I've learned to slow down and use this technology as an investment in the future of my relationships. Details may be small, but relationships are hugely important to me. I pore over my database like a tender gardener, ensuring that it's up-to-date and that I've entered current and correct information. I treat it with great care and respect because, after all, it's comprised of my Circles of Gold.

If you don't want to invest in a software system like ACT!, create your own tracking systems via Excel, Outlook, Word (in a table format) or any other system you like. LinkedIn now has the capability of allowing you to add a note which only you can see; set a reminder which will trigger an action to remind you to do something in the future; document how you and one of your connections met; and tag the person which allows you to segment them into a category or group. I have one client who is both a business wizard and an information technology guru; she is using Microsoft's Access, another database system that has tremendous capabilities.

The discipline of tracking each relationship takes time to develop and while it may seem obsessive, the practice of documenting activities, meetings and conversations along the way will save you time and trouble. There's also a great satisfaction in pulling up your database to review notes from a previous meeting and refresh your memory about what that person said, then using that information to build the relationship. There's nothing tricky or manipulative about doing this: you aren't resorting to any tactic other than supporting your memory with notes. Being able to ask someone, "How is your mom—is she doing better?" because you had a note in your database that her mom had been ill goes a long, long way in building the relationship. And the older we get, the harder it is to maintain all that random information in our heads. Let's use technology to support us *and* our Circles of Gold.

Campaign Headquarters. In order for you to accomplish your mission, you will need a space in which to work. I like to call this Campaign Headquarters or "HQ." If you run your own business, you no doubt have an office either at home or off-site that gives you the space and the tools to stay connected with people. Whatever business you're in, networking is an important strategy in keeping your business alive, so it's key to have all the tools you need to support your networking activities.

If you're employed, I recommend that you have a "shadow office" at home that mirrors your office at work. Have a duplicate copy of your contacts available to you at home as well as updated copies of your résumé, *curriculum vitae* or biography. Keep copies of project results and accomplishments on file so that you have those documents available in case you are ever severed from your employment without notice. I don't suggest this to cause you any alarm, but it's been known to happen. And I'm not suggesting that you pilfer sensitive or confidential documents from your employer. You just want to have a track record of all you've done so that if you need to go into job search mode on a moment's notice and you don't have access to your office, you have all the resources you need handy at your own "HQ."

The other reason to have your own home office is to give your networking campaign the status it deserves. Managing your career is critical. You want to have your own computer with all of your contacts loaded into a database, copies of important projects and achievements, and office supplies. Surround yourself with objects you love, whether they are works of art or photos of family and friends. Make your HQ appealing and very much your own.

Business cards. If you're employed by a company, the organization often provides you with business cards. Keep a large supply on hand and always carry some with you. I carry cards with me in a lovely leather cardholder in my purse, and I always have a back-up supply in my computer bag, at home and even in the glove box of my car. I've been known to carry cards with me on the Prairie Path where I walk with my dog or to the gym where I work out. You never know when you're going to meet someone with whom you want to stay connected.

If you're unemployed, or "between successes," have a business card made up that has your basic contact information: your name, any certifications you hold (CPA, CFP, MBA, etc.), a mailing address or P.O. box, your mobile number, and your email address. Some people add their LinkedIn address and Twitter handle. You want people to be able to find and reach you.

Often for security reasons people opt not to put a mailing address on business cards when they are unemployed or working from home, but remember that this makes it difficult for others to send you articles or thank you notes.

If you're getting business cards produced, it's appropriate to give yourself a title such as "writer" or "professional engineer," but I wouldn't get too carried away with describing what you do or want to do. Don't try to cram your résumé onto a business card. The title should remind people of who you are and what you are seeking.

I'm a purist when it comes to business cards. I think they should be simple yet elegant, on excellent paper stock (which sometimes rules out the free ones you can get online) with a matte vs. gloss finish. The highly glossy finish doesn't allow people to jot anything down, and that's a critical way to capture information following a networking call. I use people's business cards to document when and where I met them (the source of our connection), who referred me to them and any follow-up required. Of course, if it was a Circles of Gold networking conversation I'll have separate notes in a notebook. But the business card serves as an important reminder of who they are, how I know them and what I may need to do to follow up with them and keep the relationships moving.

Letterhead or note cards. You don't have to use personalized letterhead, but it's easy to order, relatively inexpensive and says a lot about you. Because I have a business, I have letterhead and note cards that were designed professionally and include my company name and logo. But you don't need to own a company in order to have your own stationery. You can acquire letterhead and note cards online, through your local printing and copy store, or at fine stationery stores. Having personalized stationery is an investment, but it also communicates several things, including that you understand the importance of correspondence, you have a brand and you're committed to staying in touch.

I also keep a stockpile of special occasion cards on hand so that I can acknowledge the people in my Circles of Gold. Whenever there's a victory to celebrate—a new job, a new baby, a marriage or life-giving divorce—I send a card. If I hear that someone has lost a loved one, I send a sympathy card. I've had several friends and clients who have lost beloved pets so I keep a supply of cards on hand that acknowledge the loss of a pet.

The older I get, the more diligent I've become about acknowledging people's birthdays. But I don't have a blanket policy to send birthday cards to clients. I personally don't like receiving birthday cards from vendors if we don't have a relationship. I also resist buying any birthday cards that make fun of people's age or are crude in any way—I figure it's better to take the high road. We're trying to build relationships here, not insult or offend people.

For my clients, I have a tradition that I've established in lieu of sending holiday cards; I send Valentine's Day cards. Because the mission of my business is to "Create a world where people love what they do and do what they love," I enjoy aligning myself with the holiday that most celebrates love. I buy small cards at Target that are bundled in groups of eight, so they aren't costly. Then I buy heart-shaped stickers to put on the outside that dress them up. The messages on the cards I choose are loving but they aren't lovey-dovey—they are often cute but not "cutesy." I've had such a great response to this tradition and was even featured recently in a blog about creative ways to connect with clients. I send these Valentine's Day cards not just to clients but also to my "posse," including my virtual assistant, my business coach, my designer, my tech guy and all the other people who help sustain my business. You may want to think of creating a tradition of your own, using your own favorite holiday as an opportunity to reach out to your Circles of Gold.

Filing system. Some of my clients are going paperless, so they don't keep actual file cabinets any more. Admittedly, I'm still attached to paper so I have file cabinets for documents related to categories such as *clients* (active and inactive), *presentations* (in development or completed); *articles and research* (on topics of interest to me, including mentoring, leadership and women in the workforce), *financials, technology,* and *association activities*. I also keep files on my computer, of course, and organize these files by client and by activity.

I think—and file—in a linear fashion, so I rarely lose track of where I stored a working file in my computer. I create files-within-files for my clients, which include meeting notes and a place for their strategic marketing plans which often are evolving. When filing documents electronically, the key is to keep your system simple and functional so that you can remember where you put a document. If necessary (and if you're working with someone else, this might be helpful), keep a master list of your files and how they are categorized in a working document to which you and others can refer.

A budget. Networking is an investment—an investment of time, energy and, in some cases, money. You want to have money earmarked for networking. This could be for chamber memberships, association dues or the cost of monthly meetings you want to attend. For instance, in the western suburbs of Chicago we have an organization called the Executives Breakfast Club. You don't have to be a member of the club to attend, but there is a cost break if you commit to a yearly membership. Not only have I heard interesting speakers, including one of my favorite authors, Tim Sanders, who wrote *Love is the Killer App: How to Win Business and Influence Friends,* but I've also made some great connections, some of which have resulted in new business. I enjoy the stimulation of the conversations of the speakers and the people at my table. And it's good practice to be in front of people, sharing my 30-second commercial as we sit around the table and introduce ourselves.

The Executives Breakfast Club was established more than 40 years ago as a forum to discuss ethics and business. They have a practice where one of the emcees poses a provocative question related to business and values, then encourages us to get up and go around the room to discuss the question with someone we don't know. For you introverts out there, that may seem like a nightmare. But it's a good way to exercise your networking muscle and we never know what kind of connections we'll make. The ticket cost is worth the investment.

Part of your budget may be earmarked for coffee dates, luncheons and the occasional rendezvous at a bar or pub. This shouldn't cost you an arm and a leg, but you do need to have cash on hand in order to pick up the check. Here's my rule of thumb: If I'm the one who made the call and suggested we get together, I'll pick up the check. I'm the one asking for their time, and in exchange for their time, I feel it's appropriate for me to pay for our refreshments or meals. A four-dollar latte is a very small price to pay for the generous gift of someone's Ideas, Opinions and Recommendations. Even a lovely lunch at a swanky restaurant is worth ten times—or maybe 100 times—the investment if that conversation is converted into an engagement or a job. So be generous when you invite people to connect with you because you are essentially "hosting" an event. You want people to feel like you've honored them and picking up the tab is one very good way to do that.

The other thing about hosting the coffee date or the meal is there is a subtle implication that you're the one in control of the meeting. You called it; you're hosting it; you're paying for it. While you may spend the majority of your time listening, you are still the one who initiated the conversation and that gives you control over the agenda. This doesn't mean you're a bully or a control freak. Think of yourself rather as a gracious host or hostess, setting the stage for a wonderful experience for your guest. Even if you're at a coffee shop, you can select a table most conducive to your conversation, order and pay for coffee and snacks and set your guest at ease in the same way you would if you were entertaining at home.

Picking up the tab also creates a context for reciprocity. When someone does something nice for us, we are conditioned to reciprocate and look for ways to do something nice for them. Don't get me wrong—you aren't buying anyone's love here. No one owes you anything, and if people graciously agree to share their IOR with you, a cup of coffee or lunch is the least you can do to express your appreciation. But there is something about being the host that puts the guest in a position to want to even the score. If your guest wants to split the bill and you insist on paying, he or she may say, "Well, I'll buy next time." Just smile and say, "That would be great." Because that implies that there will *be* a next time. And that's what networking is all about—moving the relationship forward.

The Value of Associations

You want to make sure to budget for your own professional association dues. Whether or not your company contributes to your dues, make sure you find the professional association that best fits your industry or vocation. Please don't underestimate the value of being part of your association. I was a member of the Association Forum of Chicagoland, the association for associations (everyone laughs when I tell them that); there is a hot debate among Forum executives and the broader industry about whether Millennials and Generation Xers value being affiliated with a professional association. But shrewd and strategic workers—regardless of with which generation they identify—will align themselves with the association that best reflects the trajectory of their career aspirations.

Still not convinced? Let me try to persuade you of their value:

- **Associations are ready-made networking engines.** Events, websites and programming are all designed with the members' needs in mind. You have the opportunity to connect with people who are on a similar track, including people who are ahead of you in the game and who may be able to offer informal coaching or mentoring. Some associations have formal mentoring programs, matching seasoned veterans with up-and-coming professionals. Let the association support you by connecting you with people who can advance your career.

- **If you're serious about your career, you need to be serious about your continuing education.** Professionals such as attorneys, accountants and financial planners (and many others) are required to obtain a certain amount of continuing education units in order to keep their licenses. Associations are certified to offer continuing education units and they take this responsibility seriously. Professional development is one of the primary reasons people join associations.

- **Most associations host some kind of job search function on their websites.** Employers know that they can reach targeted candidates by advertising job openings on the association website. Members can post their résumés (typically for free), so they become part of a pool of potential recruits. Some associations sponsor career fairs or devote a portion of their annual meeting to career development. For instance, the Healthcare Financial Management Association, an association with whom I'm proud to do quite a bit of work, typically has some kind of career center on-site during their huge annual convention. This is a place for people to gather, to share résumés and to get guidance from association professionals.

- **Being part of an association provides you with a platform from which to practice your business and leadership skills.** In my experience, if you show up at your association (or a Chamber of Commerce) with a smile and a positive attitude, you are eagerly embraced and encouraged to join a committee. From there, you may be tapped to become a committee chairperson—a great place for you to stretch and grow as a leader. And once you've led a committee successfully, you're now a prime candidate for a position on the association's board of directors if that's something you desire.

People become active on boards for a variety of reasons. Some are motivated to join a board of directors for professional development as well as to learn and to contribute to their professions. Those who want a board position solely for the glory of putting it on their résumés don't usually last very long. Being appointed to an association board of directors is a real privilege. You have the opportunity to sit at the table with other leaders, talking and making decisions about issues that are critical to your profession and often to your industry. I am tremendously moved, for example, by the commitment from the leaders I've seen participate in the Healthcare Financial Management Association. These people juggle the demands of their own jobs while still devoting hours of service to their association, first at the chapter level, then regionally and for some, nationally. I've interviewed many of them and they say that while they originally joined HFMA for the technical expertise it provided, they now value the *friendships and connections* they've made along the way more than anything. The most valuable part of being in the association, they say, is the networking.

- **Being part of an association can be fun.** We are by nature social animals. Associations give us opportunities to be with other people who have similar backgrounds and interests. Most associations include social activities on their calendars—mixers, fund-raisers for a good cause, golf tournaments and other opportunities to get to know each other outside the context of work. These social events bond us in a way that lasts. You get to know someone and carry that connection forward, taking the relationship to a new level. Being part of an association provides you with a ready-made group of potential friends and colleagues who likely share a passion for your profession.

- **Associations provide a pool of talented people who could become members of a potential Master Mind group in order to share best practices in your profession or industry.** People who are in the same business often face similar challenges and, instead of re-inventing the wheel, they can turn to their association colleagues to brainstorm solutions to their problems. You can form a Master Mind group—a phrase coined by the late, great author Napoleon Hill to describe a circle of peers who are each committed to each others' success. Master Mind group participants meet regularly to discuss each other's issues and challenges in confidentiality, offering Ideas, Opinions and Recommendations to help each other grow. Being part of a Master Mind Group is a brilliant way to align with peers whose ideas and energy expand possibilities for you and for every group member.

I think of associations and chambers of commerce as places to "audition." Being part of the organization gives people insights into your talents, your capabilities and your commitments. Do you show up on a regular basis? Do you contribute and volunteer where you're needed? Are you consistent in your support of the organization, whether through serving on a committee or offering sponsorships? People do business with people whom they know, and they do business with people they trust. By participating in an association, you get to demonstrate your gifts and talents, your work ethic and your commitment to the profession.

I learned about the power of associations back in the mid-1980s. In my role as manager of communications for Scottsdale Memorial Health Systems, Inc., I became involved in the Arizona Chapter of the American Society for Hospital Marketing and Public Relations, the association that aligned with my profession. Before long, I was tapped to be on the board, a responsibility for which I didn't quite feel prepared—but I agreed, knowing that the people on the board were generous and knowledgeable, and they would help me to learn.

While I was on the board I met a woman named Kyle who worked for Humana Hospital-Phoenix. (Humana later transitioned into an insurance company.) Kyle had heard through the grapevine that I was in the market for another job, and she didn't know I'd already landed at a small public relations agency in Phoenix. One day, out of the blue, I got a call from the human resources director at Humana Hospital-Phoenix. Kyle was leaving Humana and she had recommended me for her job. Although I liked my new job, I thought it would be good to at least talk to the human resources director at Humana.

Based on the strength of Kyle's recommendation, the hospital's chief executive officer welcomed me with open arms. After a cursory interview, it was clear that the job was mine if I wanted it. The salary was quite a bit higher than the job I'd just taken and the benefits were incomparable. I was thrilled to accept, and told Kyle I would be forever indebted to her for that opportunity. And it all came to pass because of a recommendation from one of my association friends.

The connections you'll make as part of an association are priceless; they will remain within your Circles of Gold for the rest of your life.

Other things to budget for include:

- **A wardrobe that screams, "I'm successful!"** I love to share stories about my first days in the work world, where women were relegated to navy blue suits with maroon bow-ties, panty hose and navy blue pumps, the required uniform that proved we were as serious about business as our male peers in their cufflinks and double-breasted suits. The workplace wardrobe has become tremendously diverse for women and men; we have many more options than we did when John Malloy's tome *Dress For Success* hit the market. Gone are those days, thank

God, although some of us love to have a good laugh about them now and then. But even though we have much more latitude about appropriate business wear, it's still important to have a wardrobe that works. You don't need a lot of money to build a wardrobe that reflects your commitment to excellence. I do a lot of my shopping at second-hand stores and the Goodwill. (Shhhh…don't tell. I prefer my audiences think I buy my designer brands at retail.)

Make sure you have items in your wardrobe that you can wear to a business meeting, a networking event, a cocktail party or business-after-hours and especially an interview. Whenever one of my clients is going on an interview, I ask what may sound like a trivial question teenagers might text to each other: "What are you wearing?" But this is an important question. I always urge my clients to wear something that makes them feel absolutely fabulous. It could be a suit but it could also be a brooch, a scarf or tie—even shoes—something that gives the client confidence and a little bit of attitude.

A dear friend, who became one of my clients, was interviewing for the position of dean of admissions at a prestigious liberal arts college. When I asked what she was wearing, she said she had a suit that she was comfortable in; she said it "would do." "Oh, no-no-no," I said gently, adding that this wasn't about being just OK with what she was wearing. She had to show up looking, and more importantly feeling, *fabulous*. My friend went out and bought a new pink suit jacket and she swears that the jacket and my coaching were the reason she got the job. Of course, that's not true—her years of experience and her many gifts and talents are why she landed the job. But looking and feeling fantastic during the interview process, especially one like hers which was grueling and involved making a presentation to a panel of academicians, was a crucial part of her success that day.

- **Technology and related resources to serve you well.** You may have guessed by now that I have a love-hate relationship with technology. I love all that it can do for us, but I hate technology when we become a slave to it or allow it to interfere with our relationships—and especially when it doesn't work. In order to wage your networking campaign, though, you need to invest in appropriate technology to maintain the relationships you're building. Smartphones allow us to check email, confirm appointments and access maps and get directions when we're on the road. Software requires upgrades. There are financial and mental costs to technology. I can handle the financial costs and, in order to free me from its psychic woes, I have a gentleman on my "posse" who handles all my technology needs. He helped me buy my most recent laptop with portability in mind. He backs up my computer on a regular basis and installs all the necessary software to ward off viruses and other malware. And he advises me when I'm considering technology purchases and upgrades. For example, when I decided to move my ACT! database to the cloud so that my assistant could work on it virtually, my tech guy assisted in evaluating the vendor and helping with the requirements to shift the information from my computer to the cloud. Could I have done this? Possibly. But that's not my area of expertise, and it requires more time and anxiety than I'd like to spend on it. As an entrepreneur, I have to be very careful about how I invest my time. And so do you!

I have a saying that I call my Diva mantra: "Don't we have people to do that?"

Do what you're best at, and hire out the rest.

Putting it All Together

We've now discussed all the elements you'll need for your networking campaign.

You have a calendar system that works and your Circles of Gold database for connecting with your contacts.

You have a tracking system that works for you, one that will help you remember where you last left off with a contact and what you need to do to move that relationship forward.

You've outfitted your office to support you and your mission—and if you're employed, you've given yourself permission to have a home office that provides you the space and resources needed to launch your campaign.

Wherever you go, you carry business cards so that at any given moment, you can make a connection and share your contact information—and you collect cards from others.

Within your cache of office supplies you have letterhead and note cards which align with you and your brand, so that you can send a letter or dash off a note to someone, including an article of interest or an expression of thanks. These will cement the bond of your connection. And you have a little stash of special occasion cards to celebrate victories, acknowledge sorrows and wish people well.

Your filing systems are in good order, both in cabinets and on your computer.

You've budgeted for your networking campaign and you have allocated funds so that you may attend events, participate in your association or chamber of commerce, stay current with technology and, of course, invest in an appropriate—and fabulous—wardrobe.

This may seem like a lot to juggle but that's the cost of becoming and staying connected. The alternative is to slog along in your current job, hoping someone will notice you and help to advance your career.

"Hope," as they say, "is not a strategy." Networking allows you to take control of your career or your business and become the driver for your own success.

13 Lather, Rinse, Repeat

The act of networking—the *joy* of networking—is not something you do only when you want or need something. Networking isn't a tactic you drag out only when you've lost a job, are unhappy with the work you're doing or need to make a quick change. That's the reason that networking gets such a bad rap: people confuse networking with "using" others to their advantage. Networking means staying connected not just when you're in transition but, really, forever. I like to say that networking is like flossing your teeth: in order for it to do any good, you have to do it all the time.

Does that sound like a life sentence to you? It shouldn't: networking is the most powerful strategy you'll ever have for making a difference in this world. We are bound to each other and there's real joy in helping others get what they want. Perhaps it's in our

DNA, but we are wired to be of service to others. And when you're excited about your mission, you get others excited, too, and they want to help. The easiest, quickest route from where you are to where you want to be is via your Circles of Gold.

The biggest mistake people make when they "land" a job is they wipe their brow and say, "Whew! Thank goodness I'm done with all that networking! Now I can focus on my job." The "job," however, is to continue to stay focused on developing one's career. And the best way to do that is to keep your network nurtured and growing. Stay engaged, keep an eye on the market, continue to help others achieve their missions and let people know you are interested in what they're doing, too.

When you are up to big things (and I know you are), networking becomes second nature to you. I learned much of what I know about the art of networking from my dad, Roger Axford. He was a professor of higher and adult education, so it's no surprise that I would grow up with the value of lifelong learning. In addition to teaching at universities, my dad often led study tours, and he taught me a lot about creating a project, then promoting it relentlessly until a goal was achieved. He was also a prolific writer and wrote numerous books—collections of inspiring biographies, books on marriage, and even a series of joke books.

Because many of his books were self-published (and this was long before independent publishing became mainstream), my dad would have his books printed and then market them himself. And by "market," I mean he would always have an abundant supply in the trunk of his white Toyota Corolla. Invariably, as he conversed with people, he would find some affinity between whomever he was speaking with and one of his books and—in the blink of an eye, he or she would be signing a check for the book which my dad by then would have cheerfully autographed. My dad taught me more than a thing or two about promotion.

Although he retired from Arizona State University, he continued to work on projects that were near and dear to him until his health precluded him from working. In the latter months of his life, I went to visit him. His "circle" had narrowed to my mom, Geri, my sister and her kids and a few close friends. There were, however, two new women in his life: his hospice nurse and the hospice case manager.

On one of the last days I spoke to him by phone, I remember saying, "Hi, Daddy. How are you today?"

"Good day," he responded in a voice that by now was weak and frail.

"Really?" I said. "What was so good about it?"

"Sold two books."

I still laugh, sometimes with tears, as I tell that story, remembering the indomitable spirit of my dad, his zest for life, and how he lived his life marketing himself and his mission and message, right up until the very end.

And that's how I want to live, connecting with others until I take my last breath. I hope you do, too.

Without taking anything away from the power and magic of networking, there is a formula, and it's a lot like the directions on a shampoo bottle: *lather, rinse, repeat*. Identify your mission. Identify your Circles of Gold. Create your 30-second commercial with a focus on your mission (not just "I need a job"), capturing the essence of what you've done, where you are now and, most importantly, what you want to do in the future to make a difference in the world. Begin having those conversations, asking people for their Ideas, Opinions and Recommendations and documenting those conversations religiously. Follow up with each and every lead. Generate as many conversations as you can—the more connections you make, the richer your campaign will be and the more results you will generate. When you've landed where you want to be, sit back for a moment, relish the victory and acknowledge the people who've supported you along the way.

Then, begin again.

14 The Gift of Gratitude

There's so much already written about the benefits of an "attitude of gratitude." We are repeatedly reminded that gratitude is a gift. Books preach the importance of gratitude, from Sarah Ban Breathnach's book *Simple Abundance: A Daybook of Comfort and Joy* to Suze Orman's books on financial freedom in which she stresses the universal law of gratitude as a principle of wealth. Perhaps you learned as a child to "count your blessings" or maybe you begin or end each day with a prayer of thanksgiving or keep a gratitude journal. Whatever your spiritual beliefs, whatever your disciplines, there's no denying that our quality of life is dependent upon approaching the world from a perspective of deep gratitude.

And that, dear reader, is the essence of networking. I'm always astonished when I hear someone say, "I didn't really get anything from that networking meeting." *Really?* Were you listening? And did the person stop what he or she was doing to meet with you and hear all about you and your mission in the world? Did they not grant you their Ideas, Opinions and Recommendations, all for the mere price of a cup of coffee? Rejoice! Celebrate! And get down on your knees, literally or figuratively, and be thankful that someone would take the time to help you along the way, as I hope you have helped others.

There's a big difference between "humility" and "humiliation." By suggesting you get down on your knees I'm not suggesting you grovel. I'm merely recommending you take the posture of deep humility, acknowledging the universe for sending you just the right person with just the right resources at exactly the right time in your life. If you didn't walk away from a networking conversation with your expectations having been met, I would ask you, "What were you expecting?" A gardener who plants a seed doesn't watch for it to sprout, but goes on to the next fertile field, sending a prayer to the heavens for a ripe harvest in the future.

I had a client, Kimberly, who was discouraged. She had had many informational interviews and even actual job interviews, but she hadn't landed a job. Kimberly confided in me, "I don't think that networking conversation worked." I smiled and added, "Yet." That word, "yet," became a code word between us and I think it's a wonderful thing for all of us to remember any time we are planting seeds for the future. Your efforts may not have netted you your desired result—yet. Give it time. Keep networking. By the way, I just learned that Kimberly, who did indeed "land," just got promoted.

When it comes to expressing our gratitude there's nothing like the good, old-fashioned thank you note. I've softened my stance on emailed thank you notes, but I prefer the "belt and suspenders" approach. That means I use both forms of communication. The email provides me with the ease of jotting off an immediate thank you for someone's time and willingness to share their IOR with me. Then I follow up with a "real" thank you note written on note cards printed with my company logo.

I've formatted my computer so that I can type my thank you notes, allowing me more space to craft a message. Then I handwrite the date and sign it with my signature, often adding a handwritten "P.S." at the top of the note, inside where it folds over. This gives it the feeling of a handwritten note but also gives me enough room to express my appreciation and reinforce my message and my mission. And I always include a business card, even if I know they have one: this reinforces my brand. I pop the note card in a red envelope that matches my logo (also part of my brand) and address it with a customized label. So the recipient sees my logo on the address label, on the business card and on the note card itself.

I sent a thank you note several years ago to a woman named Cyndi Maxey, a fellow member of the National Speakers Association. I so admire Cyndi and all that she's accomplished in her career—she's the author and co-author of several books, a certified speaking professional (CSP), a teacher and an authority on presentation skills and communication. Cyndi thanked me later for my thank you note and said something I'll never forget: "Don't ever stop doing that." Perhaps it was the way she said it—almost like, "You've got something here. Don't forget it and don't take it for granted." I took her words to heart and even carry my note cards with me when I'm on the road so I can jot off a note while I'm still in the city I'm visiting.

My mom is the one who taught me how to write a thank you note. I remember her stressing that the essence of my gratitude should be not the gift, but the thoughtfulness behind the gift. If I'm thanking someone for inviting me to their dinner party, I'll thank them for the lovely evening, not the food I consumed. I remember my mother saying, "Thank them for their hospitality, not the pork chop."

In the context of networking, you're really thanking people first of all for their *time*—that precious and irreplaceable resource they shared with you. You then want to thank them for their Ideas, Opinions and Recommendations (IOR). After all, isn't that what you were seeking and what they provided? Then you may want to add how you're going to follow up with the people or resources they shared, and make a promise to keep in touch.

Please go ahead and use technology to your advantage by sending an electronic thank you. But remember that there's nothing quite like sending a personalized thank you note. When you receive a thank you note in the mail, don't you open that first? The message, written on beautiful stationery, lifts your spirits and enlivens your day. You may prop it on a shelf for a while, relishing the good feelings that it brings, or you may store it in a treasure box, as I do, to revisit someday when life feels kind of gloomy. Just as the opposite of fear is faith, gratitude is a great antidote for the feeling of scarcity or loss. It may sound trite, but whenever you are feeling like you're missing out on things, the world hasn't been fair, or you haven't been given your due, take a moment and stop to count your blessings. If you are reading this book and poised to go to the next level in your business and career, I'm sure they are many.

Another Way to Get Unstuck

Gratitude is also a wonderful lubricant for getting "unstuck." There's something about expressing our appreciation to other people, and to the universe, that allows the floodgates to open. I had a client who was having a particularly hard time getting "in" with networking contacts. I finally asked him, "Ben, is there anyone you need to acknowledge or say 'thank you' to?" Turns out he had never acknowledged the person who opened the door that had led to his very lucrative contract, a contract that had lasted about four years. He was making good money—let's say $100,000 per year. That's a $400,000 "gift" from the friend who connected him to the company that hired him. (The guy didn't get Ben the job, but he did make it possible for Ben to get in the door, which resulted in the opportunity.)

I said, "If your friend had a key to a door and behind that door was a pile of gold coins worth $400,000, wouldn't you want to thank him for giving you that key?" I pictured the old fairy tale of Rumpelstiltskin, where the little gnome turned a pile of straw into a pile of gold. "Well, when you put it that way..." my client said. After he reconnected and thanked the person who'd helped him, floodgates of networking opportunity opened for Ben.

A Lifelong Debt

When someone is kind enough to take the time to talk with you, explore your mission and then give you his or her IOR, I believe that we owe him or her a lifelong debt of gratitude. I can never adequately thank Helen Hooper, the personnel director at Southwestern Hospital in Lawton, and our boss Tom Rine, the hospital CEO, for taking a chance on me. They saw a very young, inexperienced former reporter and gave her an opportunity to do what she did best in an industry she grew to love. My dad introduced me to the CEO of Scottsdale Memorial Health System, and although at the time I was too young to recognize the power of my Circles of Gold, I hope he knew how much I appreciated his connections. My sister-in-law, Janet McCann, interior designer extraordinaire, made the introduction that led to the job that brought my family and me to Chicago. I sent her a dozen yellow roses at the time and continue to express my appreciation to her for opening a door that changed my life. I'll never be able adequately to thank Chuck Lauer, the publisher of *Modern Healthcare* magazine, who saw something in me and recruited me to be his first director of marketing for the magazine. I'll always be indebted to Kathleen Yosko, president and CEO of Marianjoy Rehabilitation Center, for inviting me to be her vice president of marketing and build a brand new department with great and talented people; and I haven't ever forgotten the kindness of Mike McCallister, my hospital CEO and later CEO of Humana, who went to bat for me when the hospitals were sold and bought me some time with the company so I could find another job to support my family.

To whom are you indebted? Do you owe anyone a thank you note? It's never too late to thank someone, unless they've passed on. And even then, you can offer a thank you to the universe or a prayer for that person's soul. Maybe it's the person who gave you your first big break. Perhaps it's one of your teachers—I've written thank you notes to high school and middle school English teachers who encouraged me and my writing. Maybe it's our parents or the people who helped raise us who deserve a big fat "Thank you!" Reach out to them today.

Networking isn't just a verb, it's a way of life. You could even paraphrase the song from Disney's *The*

Lion King—it's the circle of life. You are surrounded by Circles of Gold. Honor those circles. Reach out to the people within them and share your mission, your dreams and your desire to make a difference. Ask them for help and be open to their IOR. Don't judge, and make sure you write everything down. Go back and thank them. And then, when the call or email comes to you and someone says, "Hey, I'm on a mission! Would you be willing to meet with me to share your ideas, opinions and recommendations?" you know what to do. Say, "Yes, I'd be delighted!" and give generously of your time, your IOR and your own Circles of Gold. That's what makes the world go around.

Remember that networking, like dancing, has a structure. Once you learn that structure—the steps, the etiquette, the tempo—you'll find you can make connections with more grace and ease than you'd ever imagined. You'll find that with practice, networking becomes effortless and even fun.

Get out there and enjoy the dance.

Acknowledgements

I'm extremely grateful to the many clients and colleagues who have helped me refine my networking philosophy. I owe a debt of gratitude to Chris Wolak, formerly of Borders, who gave me my first speaking platform. Joy Meredith supported me with encouragement, her "Me-Mapping" process and the phrase "Circles of Gold." Lesley Ronson Brown has been there for me with yoga, coffee, cocktails and everything in between. Jackie Sloane is my beloved coach—many thanks to her, to Mary Gustafson, my "book buddy" and to Katy McDonough, my "Dream Team" partner. The ladies of Panache hold me accountable monthly—thank you, Jan Faris and Maritess Bott. My "posse" gives untold support: thanks to Donna Micklich, Emma Asta, Anna Piro, Brian Karel, Mary Pat Wesche, CPA, CFP, Susan Headley, the Rev. Barb Good, Brent Ohlmann, Esq., and Sue Tripp. Joy Dooley invited me to contribute to the Community Career Center in Naperville, IL, where my coaching practice was born, and Jim Fergle keeps asking me back to workNet DuPage. My friends from the National Speakers Association have cheered me on *and* kicked me in the pants— thanks to Steve Beck, Conor Cunneen and the whole NSA-IL board & membership. To my writing buddies and groups throughout the years—Jennifer Delahunty, Ellie Waterson, the spirit of Brenda Felldin, Jan Kelly and Rita Emmett—many thanks. Dwight and Colleen Olson gave me time at their idyllic brownstone in Brooklyn to complete my manuscript; Jennifer Grant was the world's best editor; and Becky Lemna shared her amazing gift of design. My beloved parents were the benefactors of this project. My brother, Scott, taught me how to live lightly and my sister, Naida, taught me the importance of listening and two coats of mascara. And most of all, to Bill, Kitty and Widge— you are the diamonds that sparkle in my Circles of Gold.

About the Author

Vickie Austin is a business and career coach and a professional speaker. Her company, CHOICES Worldwide, is based in Wheaton, IL. She attended Arizona State University where she graduated *magna cum laude* with a bachelor's degree in English literature and she received an executive master's degree in international management from Thunderbird School of Global Management. Vickie is active in the Illinois chapter of the National Speakers Association and has served as Dean of the Speakers Academy for aspiring professional speakers. She and her husband Bill, an artist, have two grown children, Kitty and Will. Vickie and Bill live in Wheaton with their dog, Peanut Butter, a slightly off terrier with a penchant for chewing on fuzzy bedroom slippers.

You can reach Vickie at vaustin@choicesworldwide.com and read her blog at http://vickieaustin.com.

Printed in Great Britain
by Amazon